DISCOVERING THE
NORTH YORK MOORS

Discovering the North York Moors

Its Hidden Places, Curiosities and Strange Events

with Malcolm Boyes & Hazel Chester

First published in 1996 by

Smith Settle Ltd
Ilkley Road
Otley
West Yorkshire
LS21 3JP

ISBN 1 85825 041 2

All photographs are by the authors, with the exception of those on
pages 10 and 85 (bottom) which are from the Malcolm Boyes Collection.

British Library Cataloguing-in-Publication Data:
A catalogue record is available for this book
from the British Library.

Opening page: Malo Cross
Title page: Roseberry Topping.

Set in Souvenir

Designed, printed and bound by
SMITH SETTLE
Ilkley Road, Otley, West Yorkshire LS21 3JP

Contents

Historic Cleveland

The Cleveland Hills

The Upper Esk Valley

The Hambleton Hills

The Southern Dales

Gateway to the Moors

Heart of the Moors

Introduction

There is no finer place to be in August and September when the heather blooms than on the North York Moors. The rich purple carpet of heather seen on the lofty ridges that cross the moors gives way to small dales fields and tree-fringed riverbanks as you descend into the valleys. At other times of the year it is quieter, especially in the coastal villages and towns. In winter the views from the ridges can be clearer and more extensive, while in spring the wild daffodils bloom around Farndale, and the hedges and trees burst into life. Largely untouched by massive twentieth century developments, the villages of the North York Moors retain many interesting treasures that have been swept away in other places.

For the walker who wishes to pull on his boots and get away from traffic jams, there is a road walked by Roman soldiers and another that has disappeared altogether unless a diligent search is made. There are about 1,500 standing stones and crosses to discover on the moors. Some are boundary markers between parishes or estates; others have acted like modern road signs indicating the direction to travellers. The tales behind a few of these stones are recalled in the following pages.

The area is rich in castles and medieval monastic houses, many of which have interesting stories to tell. A wealth of treasures can also be found in the local museums — souvenirs of special occasions, and tools and utensils recalling how people have lived in this area over many centuries. It is only 150 years ago that the moorland villages were remote and cut off from urban life. It was a time when families would sit round a peat fire on a winter evening and tales would be handed down through the family of witches, folklore and local superstitions.

The 100 places of interest described in this book have been arranged in ten sections. Each section would make a day-long excursion onto the moors, possibly with a stop for lunch or an evening meal before returning home. A simple schematic map at the beginning of each section gives the locations of the sites in relation to one another, and an overall map of the moors (overleaf) means you can see at a glance if the town, village or area which you are visiting holds something of interest. The reference numbers used in all the maps and index refer to the page on which the particular item appears.

At some places you may only spend ten minutes visiting an inscribed stone or memorial plaque; at other places you may spend an hour or two visiting an abbey or museum. We have not given opening times for places as they are subject to change, so please check with the local Tourist Information Centre.

A rough description is given as to where each place is situated, as well as a six figure grid reference which precisely pinpoints the place. All Ordnance Survey maps carry a description of how to calculate a grid reference on to the map. The easiest map to use is the Ordnance Survey Touring map of the North York Moors, and where appropriate this is indicated at the end of the grid reference. If the place is outside the range of the map, an Ordnance Survey Landranger map is indicated. For more detail you can use the 1:25,000 Outdoor Leisure series which covers the area in the eastern and western sheets. All grid references are the same whichever map you use.

Malcolm Boyes & Hazel Chester
Norton, Malton
April 1996

Overall Map of the North York Moors

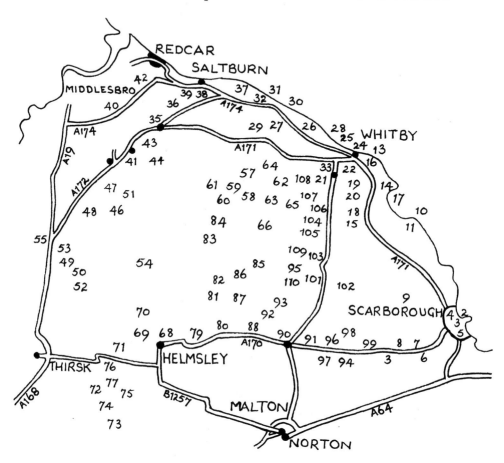

Round and About Scarborough

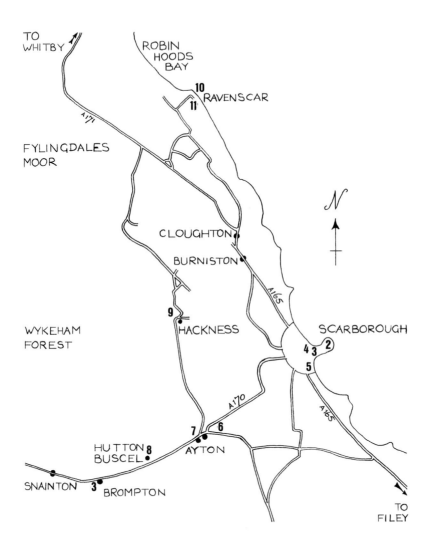

A Scarborough Warning

Separating the two bays in Scarborough is the lofty headland on which stands the castle. The castle is in the care of English Heritage and offers magnificent sea views from the grounds. A curtain wall and steep cliffs gave protection around the greater part of the grounds, and the landward side was defended by a massive gatehouse. Similar castles have withstood sieges for months, yet Scarborough Castle was taken in one afternoon.

In 1554, Thomas, the son of Sir Thomas Stafford, infiltrated the castle on market day with a group of men who were all disguised as local countryfolk. At a given signal they overpowered guards and took the gates, admitting more of their men. The surprise assault gave them possession of the castle. Three days later a strong force retook the castle and the leaders were later executed. The action became the source of ballads which mention a Scarborough Warning, a warning and an attack but the attack comes first!

Site: Castle Road, Scarborough.

Grid Ref: TA 049891 (Scarborough & Bridlington Landranger 101)

That Magnificent Man

The man looked upon as the Father of Aeronautics is not one of the Montgolfier Brothers, whose balloon first took to the air over Paris in 1783. Nor is it Wilbur or Orville Wright who designed and built Flyer I, the first successful powered aircraft. The title has been given to Sir George Cayley, who was born in Paradise House close to St Mary's Church in Scarborough in 1773, where the event is recorded by a plaque.

He spent most of his life at Brompton, between Scarborough and Pickering, and designed a number of 'flying devices'. He designed the first moveable tailplane to control flight and a wheeled under-carriage. In 1853 the first man-carrying flight in a heavier-than-air machine as opposed to balloons took place at Brompton. The choice of first aviator fell to Sir George Cayley's coachman, who glided across the valley then immediately offered to resign from the post. The only problem then was that there was no engine available light enough to power an aircraft.

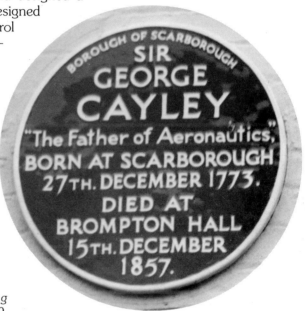

Site: Paradise House, 70 yards (65m) to the left of St Mary's Church, Scarborough, when facing the sea. Brompton is on the A170 Scarborough–Pickering road.

Grid Refs: Paradise House TA 048890. Brompton Hall SE 940822 (both places are on (Scarborough & Bridlington Landranger 101)

Where Acton Bell is Buried

In May 1849 two sisters and a close friend journeyed to Scarborough from the West Riding and took lodgings at No 2 the Cliff. They were all aware that one of the sisters was terminally ill with consumption, but had travelled to Scarborough at the sick girl's request so she could enjoy looking out of the window at the sea. On the 28th May she died, aged only twenty-nine, and was buried in Scarborough churchyard.

Her grave is now the most visited one in the churchyard. She had two books published under the pseudonym of Acton Bell, but the world now knows that the young lady was Anne Brontë, the only member of the famous literary family buried away from Haworth. Her companions on this last journey were her sister Charlotte and friend Ellen Nussey. In less than a year Charlotte had lost her brother, Branwell, and her two sisters, Anne and Emily.

Site: St Mary's churchyard, Castle Road, Scarborough.

Grid Ref: TA 047890 (Scarborough & Bridlington, Landranger 101)

A Room with a View!

Lying off Filey Road in Scarborough is a small free car park with excellent views across the South Bay to Scarborough Castle. Near the entrance to the car park is an information board giving details of the Holbeck Hall Hotel which stood on the site. On the morning of the 4th June 1993 the guests awoke to find that doors and windows were sticking and the rose gardens had disappeared into the sea overnight. A huge landslip had carried away thousands of tons of rock and soil.

Over the next week the cliff continued to slip away, and the four-star hotel slowly crumbled as its foundations gave way. Thousands of people came to watch as the hotel collapsed room by room. The conservatory, which offered sea views to guests, went during the first day; a week later over half the hotel had gone and lay strewn across the foot of the cliffs. The next time you ask for a room with a sea view, remember the Holbeck Hall Hotel!

Site: off the A165 Scarborough–Bridlington road about one mile (1.5km) from Scarborough town centre. Turn left along Sea Cliff Road to the car park.

Grid Ref: TA 048868 (Scarborough & Bridlington Landranger 101)

Those Industrious Bees

Heather honey is famous, and to obtain this distinctive flavour in the late nineteenth and early twentieth century, many hives were transported onto the North York Moors for August and September when the heather bloomed.

The place to see bees at work producing honey is at the award-winning Honey Farm at East Ayton. There is free access to the gift shop, craft shop, restaurant and farm shop, but there is a fee for the fascinating guided tour of the hives.

This is something that will appeal to people of all ages and should not be missed. You can watch the industrious bees flying in and out of the hives through vents in the roof while you are safely behind glass. As well as the traditional wooden hives and straw skeps, there are bee colonies producing honey in a tree trunk, a doll's house and a letter box, each of which can be swung open to reveal the bees and combs of honey. Your guide will be an experienced bee keeper who will answer all your questions and encourage you to count the 60,000 bees in a summer colony.

Site: at Betton Farm on the A170 Scarborough to East Ayton road.

Grid Ref: SE 999854 (North York Moors Touring map)

A Country Residence

Set in the middle of a field close to the River Derwent are the remains of Ayton Castle, at one time the home of the Evers Family. Sir Ralph Evers was appointed governor of Scarborough Castle by Henry VIII. He defended the besieged castle during the Pilgrimage of Grace in 1536, for twenty days the garrison surviving on bread and water. He was succeeded at Scarborough Castle by Lord William Evers.

The tranquil setting of Ayton Castle would be a complete change from the busy life of Scarborough.

A footpath past the castle leads into Forge Valley where the infant River Derwent cuts its way through a narrow wooded gorge. This is a national nature reserve, and while it may take only a few minutes to view Ayton Castle, an hour or two can be spent identifying the plants and birds in this delightful valley. There are plenty of chaffinches and tits, and you may also see nuthatch, treecreeper, greater spotted woodpecker and the more elusive green woodpecker.

Site: walk up Yedmandale road in West Ayton, turn right along Castle Rise and follow the footpath to Ayton Castle.

Grid Ref: SE 987850 (North York Moors Touring map)

A Home for Stray Cattle

The stone-built houses of Hutton Buscel stand on a hillside overlooking the Scarborough to Pickering road. Opposite the church is Great Moor Lane, leading up onto the former moors which are now covered in forestry. To the left of the road is a circular stone-walled enclosure with a gate sealing off the only opening. This was the manorial pinfold which was restored in 1981

In earlier times the pinfold was used to impound cattle, sheep, goats or other farm animals found straying around the village or the lanes. Each parish or manorial court appointed a pinder or poundkeeper who was responsible for impounding the animals. The owner had then to approach the pinder and pay a fine to redeem his animals. In those days it paid you to keep your fences in good order. There are other restored

pinfolds at Snainton (SE 917824), Goathland — inset — (NZ 826005) and Hutton le Hole (SE 704902).

Site: 150 yards (135m) along Great Moor Road, Hutton Buscel, which is five miles (8km) south-west of Scarborough

Grid Ref: SE 971842 (North York Moors Touring map)

A Mysterious Stream

The small village of Hackness stands below delightful wooded hillsides close to the infant River Derwent. The site was chosen for a Celtic nunnery connected to Whitby Abbey in the seventh century. On the death of St Hilda of Whitby, one of the nuns dreamed of the event and told the other nuns hours before the news arrived. A later Benedictine monastery was founded in the eleventh century on the site of the present interesting church.

Across the road from the church entrance is a small stream. Walk upstream beside the road and you will see the stream disappear under the support of a bridge. At the other side there is no sign of a stream! Is it a spring that comes to the surface at that point or is it piped underground — but why start a stream under a bridge support? It is only a short stream and you can walk the other way to reach the point where it joins Lowdales Beck on its journey to merge with the River Derwent.

Site: near Hackness Church on the unclassified road from East Ayton to Burniston, five miles (8km) west of Scarborough.

Grid Ref: SE 969905 (North York Moors Tourist map)

The Do-it-Yourself Rescue

It was a dark winter's night in 1913 as the 3,290 ton steamship *Coronation* headed across the North Sea from Bremen to Sunderland. A south-easterly gale was blowing the ship off course as she was carrying only ballast. In the early hours of the morning, with a snow storm raging, the ship ran aground near Ravenscar. The crew fired their distress flares but because of the 600 feet (183m) high cliffs and the snow storm, the stranding went unnoticed.

Undaunted, the crew launched the ship's boat and six volunteers rowed ashore with a lifeline. A bosun's chair was erected and through the crew's own efforts they reached dry land. The following morning the people of Ravenscar were amazed to see the stranded ship.

The village has wide-ranging views across Robin Hood's Bay from its vantage point to the south. Just beyond the Raven Hall Hotel, a path leads to the cliff tops where 600 feet (180m) below is the site where the *Coronation* was stranded.

Site: Ravenscar, 10 miles (16km) north of Scarborough.

Grid Ref: NZ 983017 (North York Moors Touring map)

The Village that Never Was

The railway line from Scarborough to Whitby was one of the most scenic in Britain. It was opened in 1885, and ten years later the virtues of the area around Ravenscar were being promoted by Ravenscar Estate Company. Valuable freehold building plots were for sale. There was fine bracing air, plenty of moorland walks, golf links and magnificent sea views. The Raven Hall Hotel also had cliff terraces and hanging gardens. Rail excursions were run from the West Riding and anyone buying a plot had their fare refunded.

Very few building plots were sold. The fact that the sea was 600 feet (180m) below the township with no easy access may have influenced some buyers. In winter the conditions can become Arctic. The building plots were laid out between Station Square and the Raven Hall Hotel, but the idea never reached fruition.

Site: follow the road through Ravenscar, turning right at the Raven Hall Hotel to Station Square.

Grid Ref: NZ 983014 (North York Moors Touring map)

Whitby's Hinterland

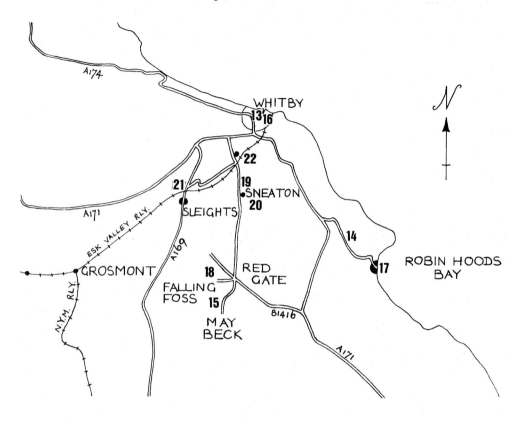

The Lasting Penance

In the middle of the twelfth century a party of local gentry were on a wild boar hunt in the woods near Whitby. The wild boar sought refuge at a hermitage in the woods, and the hermit closed the door, leaving the baying hounds on the other side. The furious gentlemen broke into the hermitage and their action mortally wounded the hermit.

Now in fear of their lives, they fled but were brought back to the Abbot of Whitby. The men were forgiven by the dying hermit provided they plant in Whitby Harbour a hedge of stakes, cut with a penny knife from a copse. The penance was to take place at nine o'clock on Ascension Eve (forty days after Good Friday), if the tide permits. The hedge must be built strong enough to withstand three tides, and at high tide the hedge is submerged. A plaque fixed to the railings on Church Street records the site of the event, which still takes place each year.

Site: Church Street, nearly opposite Salt Pan Steps, Whitby.

Grid Ref: NZ 902106 (North York Moors Touring map)

T' Awd Abba Well

Standing beside the road from High Hawsker to Robin Hood's Bay is a small brick building whose roof is formed from two large, roughly carved stone slabs. This is known in the local dialect as T' Awd Abba Well (The Old Abbey Well). On the side away from the road is a doorway which opens to reveal the reservoir of water. It has been used by the local community since the twelfth century as a source of good drinking water. In the early nineteenth century its water was carted to a reservoir near Whitby Abbey, from where it could be piped to the houses on the east side of the River Esk.

The well is also called the Boiling Well. This may be a reference to times when the spring at this point forced so much water to the surface that it appeared to boil.

Site: four miles (6.5km) south-east of Whitby beside the B1447 High Hawsker to Robin Hood's Bay road.

Grid Ref: NZ 937068 (North York Moors Touring map)

Nature's Wonderland

From Red Gate, set on the moors south of Sneaton, two roads lead down to car parks set in idyllic countryside. The first road, which passes through the red-painted gates, descends to May Beck. From here there is a delightful walk around the May Beck Farm Trail, a waymarked trail of some four miles visiting moorland and streamside paths.

Another waymarked trail follows May Beck to Midge Hall, where there is the sixty-seven foot (21m) high Falling Foss waterfall. This waterfall can be more easily approached by taking the road from Red Gate that leads to Newton House. Close by there is a woodland car park. There are a number of tracks wandering through this sylvan wonderland to delight visitors.

Site: Red Gate is on the B1416 some 4 miles (6.5km) south of Whitby and two miles (3.25km) south of Sneaton.

Grid Ref: NZ893047 (North York Moors Touring map)

A Quaint and Wonderful Church

Whether or not you are the type of person who enjoys looking around churches, St Mary's Church at Whitby will fascinate you. It is set on the cliff top overlooking the harbour. To reach the church from the town you have to climb the 199 Steps, a penance

in itself. Inside the church are many box pews, some listing the names of nearby villages whose inhabitants could sit in these places.

The vicar has a three-decker pulpit from which to preach. One incumbent had a deaf wife, and so to enable her to listen to the sermon he installed a long ear trumpet beside the pulpit. The church furnishings include an upper gallery which may have been built and installed by the town's shipwrights. In the entrance is the memorial to the 1861 Lifeboat Disaster, when twelve of the thirteen man crew of the rowing lifeboat were drowned while attempting their sixth rescue of the day.

Site: at the top of the 199 Steps on the east side of Whitby.

Grid Ref: NZ 901112 (North York Moors Touring map)

We'll Launch from Bay

On the stormy night of the 18th January 1881 the brig *Visitor* sought shelter in Robin Hood's Bay. At daybreak the wrecked boat was discovered with its crew sheltering in a boat to the leeward. A message was sent to Whitby, but the high seas prevented the rowing lifeboat leaving the harbour.

The bold decision was made to launch the boat straight into Robin Hood's Bay. The six mile (9.5km) journey involved hauling the lifeboat up to 550 feet (165m) before it could begin the descent to sea level. The roads were blocked by a few feet of snow.

Undeterred, some sixty people began clearing the road while horses began to haul the carriage. As word went round this grew to 200 men and eighteen horses, while a similar number cleared the route into Bay Town. After three and a half hours' work the lifeboat was launched into the bay. At the first attempt the rough seas smashed six oars. At the second attempt, with a crew of eighteen instead of twelve, the lifeboat succeeded in rescuing the shipwrecked crew. A bold decision had paid off.

Site: a memorial stands at the top of the Bank, Robin Hood's Bay.

Grid Ref: NZ 951052 (North York Moors Touring map)

The Hermitage

Places called the Hermitage usually fall into one of two categories: either they are genuine places where a hermit lived; or they were established as part of some landscaping scene in the eighteenth and nineteenth centuries where people could retire to for some solitude. The Hermitage below Newton House falls into the latter category.

A massive single boulder has been carved into a rock shelter with an internal seat capable of seating about ten people. There are two more seats set on the top of the rock. At the other side of the path is a belvedere or viewpoint looking out through the trees over the extensively wooded valley of Little Beck. The Hermitage is passed on the

190 mile (304km) long Coast to Coast walk from St Bees Head in Cumbria to Robin Hood's Bay. If you follow the walk northwards towards Littlebeck you pass through an area were alum was quarried.

Site: from the Falling Foss car park (NZ 889037), pass through a gap in the wall opposite the entrance and follow the red marked trail for about half a mile (0.8km).

Grid Ref: NZ 885040 (North York Moors Touring map)

The Monks' Trod

Scattered over the North York Moors are stone causeways which mark out routes once well used by travellers many centuries ago. Over the years, with the hooves of packhorse animals constantly tramping over them, they became worn. Someone decided that if they turned the stones over they would last for a few more centuries. When they lifted the stones, they found that someone had already turned the well-worn stones a few centuries earlier!

It has been a puzzle as to who paid for the stones to be laid in the first place. Was it the wealthy medieval abbeys wanting to improve transportation for their own goods across the inhospitable and boggy moors? No one knows. The Monks' Trod north of Sneaton is a line of flagged stones which extend for over half a mile down to Shawn Riggs Beck and on towards Larpool Hall. In places where the path descends, upright stones act as a brake for the horses' hooves.

Site: follow the signed 'Footpath to Whitby' in Sneaton, 2 miles (3.25km) south of Whitby off the B1416.

Grid Ref: NZ 895077 (North York Moors Touring map)

Sneaton Beacon

As the road through the village of Sneaton becomes a country lane, you can see a pair of tall poles on your right holding aloft a metal basket. In the late sixteenth century, and again during the late eighteenth century, the villagers of Sneaton would cast an anxious eye towards the beacon and be reassured that it remained unlit.

A constant watch would be kept on a set of beacons at Whitby, for if the Spanish Armada was sighted or, two centuries later, the Napoleonic Invasion took place, the beacon at Whitby would be lit. Sneaton would then light their beacon, which could be seen at Danby Beacon some ten miles (16km) to the west. More beacons would be lit further inland to alert the military forces and the militia — fortunately on neither occasion was the beacon lit, much to the relief of the folk in Sneaton.

Site: at the east end of Sneaton village, two miles (3.25km) south of Whitby.

Grid Ref: NZ 898076 (North York Moors Touring map)

Featherbed Lane

What was known as the narrowest king's highway in Britain climbs from Briggswath to Aislaby, but not a lot of people know that. In fact not a lot of people know where Briggswath is situated. The summer motorist from Pickering to Whitby who descends steep Blue Bank from the moors into Sleights and then begins his climb back out from the River Esk — that is when he touches the edge of Briggswath. It is the village on the north side of the river, established around the ancient ford and bridge over the River Esk.

A signpost now indicates Featherbed Lane, a narrow opening between the gardens of houses. Once you set off up the track you realise its age. The flagged path has been in use for centuries and you will believe that there are no highways any narrower. The path climbs steeply out of the valley, crosses the modern road and continues upwards to the village of Aislaby, where there are splendid views over the lower Esk Valley.

Site: on the B1410 Sleights to Ruswarp road in Briggswath.

Grid Ref: NZ 868082 (North York Moors Touring map)

The £1 Bridge

'Psst — want to buy five million bricks for a quid?' This was the offer that was being made in early 1992, and not by a spiv but the respectable British Railways Property Board. Striding across the Esk Valley at Larpool, near Whitby, is the viaduct that carried the Whitby–Scarborough railway line. For your £1 you received ownership of the bridge composed of five million bricks and the cost of maintaining the structure.

It took two years between 1882 and 1884 to construct the viaduct and cost about £40,000. The railway journey from Whitby to Scarborough was one of the most scenic in Britain. The coastal views were all on the left side, so you had to get a right-hand-side seat at Whitby Station because the engine hauled the carriages up to Whitby West Cliff, then changed ends for the journey across the viaduct and down the coast, a point that caught many travellers by surprise.

Site: best seen on the descent of Ruswarp Bank, or by taking the footpath to Whitby from Ruswarp for 200 yards (180m).

Grid Ref: NZ 895096 (North York Moors Touring map)

The Heritage Coast

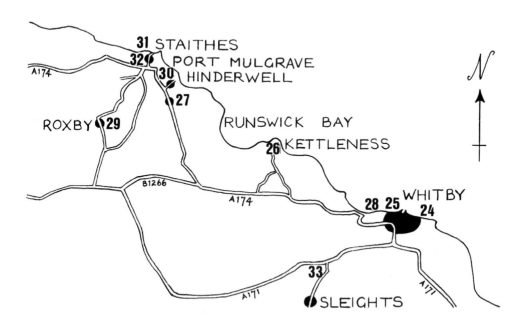

24 The *Rohilla* disaster
25 Captain Cook's statue, Whitby
26 Vanished village of Kettleness
27 St Hilda's Well, Hinderwell
28 Sandsend's alum trail

29 Horseshoe Forge, Roxby
30 Port Mulgrave
31 Cod and Lobster Inn, Staithes
32 Staithes bonnets
33 Plaque to first German aircraft shot
      down in WWII

The Rohilla *Disaster*

The Rohilla Monument in Whitby Cemetery records the names of ninety-one officers and men who died when the hospital ship *Rohilla* struck a mine at 4.10 on the morning of Friday the 30th October 1914, then ran aground at Saltwick Nab, south of Whitby. The miracle is that 138 people were rescued in scenes of heroism rarely equalled. The rowing lifeboat could not get out of the harbour due to a gale, so Whitby folk hauled the boat along the base of the cliffs and seventeen lives were saved. Dragging the boat back for a second attempt, they rescued a further eighteen before the boat was smashed by the rising tide.

Scarborough's rowing lifeboat was towed by tug to the scene, but couldn't approach due to high seas and returned after sixteen hours at sea. Meanwhile some of the crew were attempting to swim ashore and a round-the-clock vigil was kept to haul them to safety. Finally the Tynemouth motor lifeboat came down the coast and accomplished a dramatic rescue of the remaining crew of fifty.

Site: Whitby Cemetery, off the road to Larpool and Ruswarp. Walk straight through the cemetery and the archway, and the monument to ninety-one officers and men who died and the grave of thirty-three bodies is on the left.

Grid Ref: NZ 902097 (North York Moors Touring map)

James Cook's Statue

Standing on Whitby's West Cliff is a statue to James Cook, who served his apprenticeship as a seaman in the harbour below. In Resolution Park, Anchorage, in Alaska is an identical statue taken from a mould of the Whitby statue. James Cook explored the Alaskan coastline in 1778 on his third great voyage of exploration.

Cook was a man who skilfully navigated and charted many coastlines, and monuments have been erected to him all over the world. In British Columbia there are ones around Nootka Sound and overlooking Victoria Harbour. In Queen Charlotte's Sound, New Zealand, which James Cook used as a southern base on five occasions, there is a monument beside the beach where he serviced his ships. There are numerous memorials to him along Australia's east coast, including the first laser beam lighthouse built on Point Danger. A project of which he would have approved.

Site. West Cliff, Whitby.

Grid Ref. NZ 897114 (North York Moors Touring map)

The Vanished Village

The hamlet of Kettleness consists of one or two farms and cottages and the former railway station. One hundred and seventy years ago it was a thriving community with John Birks running the Anchor Inn. The men worked at the alum quarries and in the alum works. This was where the shale was burnt. The ash was then placed in settling tanks and mixed with urine; after three days the liquid was drawn off and heated, the resulting crystals being the alum.

On the night of the 17th December 1829 the cliff gave way and slid into the sea, taking the village along with it. The inhabitants rushed from their homes, but in the darkness it was some time before they realised what was happening and could see if everyone was safe. They made their way down to the sea and attracted the attention of the alum boat *Henry* which was lying offshore, and they spent the night sheltering on board the boat. It was two years before the alum works were operating again.

There are excellent coastal walks along the Cleveland Way and you can look down on the extensively quarried headland.

Site: the village is signposted off the A174 Whitby to Saltburn road
Grid Ref: NZ 830156 (North York Moors Touring map)

St Hilda's Well

The village of Hinderwell takes its name from the well in the churchyard. This well has provided water for the inhabitants for many years and is named after St Hilda, the abbess of the Celtic monastery at Whitby who died in AD 680. Behind the church, a set of stone flags lead down to the well. The stone well carries a plaque recording its restoration by Hilda Palmer of Crinkle Park in 1912.

Traditionally the local schoolchildren used to come to the well on Ascension Day (forty-one days after Good Friday). They would place liquorice in bottles and fill them up with water. The liquorice would permeate the water, adding a taste. This children's drink was called Spanish, and Spanish Water Day was an event which took place at many holy wells through out England.

Site: eight miles (13km) north-west of Whitby on the A174; the church is at the northern end of the village.

Grid Ref: NZ 791170 (North York Moors Touring map)

Sandsend's Alum Trail

Sandsend Ness is the headland that juts out at the north-western end of the long stretch of beach which begins at Whitby. The headland was quarried for alum during the eighteenth and nineteenth century. The valuable chemical was used in leather tanning and for paper making. Cement and sandstone were also commercially extracted.

The 2 mile (3.25km) long Sandsend Trail begins from the car park where the alum works used to stand. A flight of steps lead up to the former railway line used by the Whitby, Redcar and Middlesbrough Union Railway, which opened in 1883 and closed in 1958. On your left at the top of the flight of stairs you can see the former Sandsend railway station. A nature trail guide which can be obtained locally gives details of the quarries and layers of sandstone, alum shale and cement shale, as well as the rich variety of flora and fauna and fossils that may be encountered on the walk.

Site: start from the car park at the foot of Lythe Bank in Sandsend, 2½ miles (4km) north-west of Whitby.

Grid Ref: NZ 860129 (North York Moors Touring map)

The Horseshoe Forge

When many people were illiterate, tradesmen displayed their products with signs outside the door, a tradition that still flourishes with inn signs. The traveller passing through the village of Roxby would have no difficulty recognising the village blacksmith if he wanted his horse shoeing. In the centre of a row of stone houses is the smithy and the entrance is in the shape of a massive horseshoe.

Inscribed above the horseshoe are the words Turton Cottages and the date 1858. It was designed by George Goldie, an architect who was better known for his work on Catholic churches. It was built for the Turton Estate. There is a similar blacksmith's shop at Upsall on the western edge of the North York Moors.

Site: 2¹/₂ miles (4km) south-west of Staithes on the road to Scaling Reservoir.

Grid Ref: NZ 764156 (North York Moors Touring map)

The Port with No Roads

Standing on the cliff top at the village of Port Mulgrave, you can view the spectacular coastal scenery. Some 300 feet (90m) below you is the sea, and tucked into the corner of the small bay are what remains of two harbour arms which are used for protection by a few boats. The port was a busy place between 1860 and 1916, as iron ore was shipped out of the harbour and taken up to Jarrow on the Tyne for smelting. Looking around the steep cliffs, you may wonder how the iron ore reached the harbourside.

The first iron mine opened on the cliff top in 1857 and the ore was lowered down an incline. Later a 135 foot (41m) deep shaft was used to drop the ore and then it was taken by a tunnel to the harbour. This mine closed in 1880, but five years earlier the Grinkle Mine opened some two miles (3.25km) to the west. A narrow-gauge railway carried the iron ore through two tunnels and across three bridges to emerge beside the harbour at Port Mulgrave.

Site: take the road behind the church in Hinderwell on the A174 nine miles (14.5km) north-west of Whitby.

Grid Ref: NZ 799176 (North York Moors Touring map)

The Cod and Lobster Inn

Standing in a prominent position on the harbourside at Staithes is the Cod and Lobster Inn. The inn was serving fishermen as they worked around the harbour before 1820 when Matthew Trattles was the innkeeper, a position he still maintained in 1840. It was then estimated that some 400 men and boys in the village were working in the fishing industry. Being in such an exposed position, facing the sea, the inn has been damaged or destroyed on a number of occasions.

The last time was in the disastrous East Coast Floods of the 31st January 1953. A storm surge driven by northwesterly winds swept down the North Sea coast from Scotland to the Thames Estuary, breaching sea defences. Over 300 people lost their lives along the east coast of England. At the Cod and Lobster the kitchen, the scullery and two bedrooms on the seaward side were swept into the harbour, along with the entire bottled stock. For months afterwards the locals were recovering the bottles from the sand. The walls of the inn which face the sea are now 14 inches (350mm) thick and reinforced with steel rods.

Site: Staithes is signposted off the A174 Whitby to Saltburn road.

Grid Ref: NZ 782188 (North York Moors Touring map)

Staithes Bonnets

Walk down into the cramped village of Staithes on a misty autumn day and you could easily imagine yourself stepping back over a century to a time when this village was one of the most profitable on the east coast of England. In the 1840s there were over eighty boats operating out of the harbour. The larger ones were manned by seven men, the rest had a crew of either three or four.

Once the men returned with their catch, the fishermen's wives would set to mending the nets, attaching to the lines the bait they had collected earlier and moving the catch to the auction place or for salting. Much of the catch and lines were carried on the head, so to protect the hair and prevent the wet slime running down the back of the neck the

women wore a distinctive bonnet. They were traditionally made from white lawn, a type of fine linen, but a newly widowed woman wore a black bonnet, later changing to a lilac bonnet for 'half mourning'. The best time to see the traditional bonnets being worn is on special occasions in the village like the August Lifeboat Day.

Site: Staithes lies just off the A174 Whitby to Saltburn road.

Grid Ref: NZ 784187 (North York Moors Touring map)

A German Raider

At the point above Sleights where the A169 from Pickering meets the A171 from Whitby to Guisborough, there are stone pillars on either side of the road. On the western one is a plaque recording the shooting down of the first enemy aircraft in England during the Second World War. This took place on the 3rd February 1940.

The radar station set high on the moors near Danby Beacon detected an unidentified aircraft some sixty miles (100km) out to sea. Fighter aircraft from Acklington in Northumberland were scrambled and they headed south at just above sea level. When they arrived off Whitby they found the aircraft attacking shipping. Before the Heinkel could seek the cover of the low cloud base, Flight Lieutenant Peter Townsend (later romantically linked with Princess Margaret) lined up the aircraft in his sights and scored a hit. It crashed eighty yards (73m) north of the plaque.

Site: at the junction of the A171 and A169 roads two miles (3.25km) west of Whitby.

Grid Ref: NZ 869098 (North York Moors Touring map)

Historic Cleveland

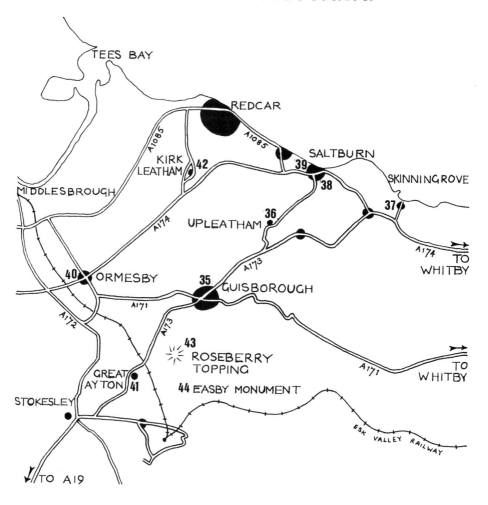

A Workman's Accident

Towering above the skyline of Guisborough is the stonework of the east end of the Augustinian priory. What must have been a majestic building was built in the fourteenth century after two disasters. Walter Hemingford, canon of Guisborough in 1289, records that a vile plumber with his two workmen burnt the church while soldering up two holes in the old lead with fresh pewter. With a wicked disposition he had placed crucibles and charcoal on the roof along with dry wood and turf — presumably to melt the pewter. At noon he descended, thinking his workmen had put out the fire, but embers of charcoal re-ignited and set the roof on fire. The church was engulfed in flames, and vestments, theological books and nine valuable chalices were lost.

The second church suffered at the hands of Scottish raiders between 1327 and 1377 during the reign of Edward III, and in 1375 a licence was granted to fortify and embattle the priory. Today you can see the magnificent east end and many of the foundations of the building, which is in the care of English Heritage.

Site: in the centre of Guisborough, 8 miles (13km) south-east of Middlesbrough.

Grid Ref: NZ 616160 (North York Moors Touring map)

Yorkshire's Smallest Church

York Minster is the largest medieval church in Britain. At the other end of the scale is the old St Andrew's Church, which stands about halfway between the villages of Upleatham and Skelton Beck. It dates back to Norman times and was later given to Guisborough Priory. The tower was added in 1684. The present tiny stone-built church with its tiled roof is 17 feet 9 inches long by 13 feet wide (5.5m x 4m) and originally formed the western end of the Norman nave. It has a capacity of twelve people.

The Norman font was taken to the new church built in Upleatham in the nineteenth century. It is a miracle that the old church still survives, as the necessary powers were obtained in 1822 to demolish the building. From the churchyard there is a pleasant view over the fields and wooded river valley to the North Sea.

Site: beside the B1268 Guisborough to Saltburn road, 2½ miles (4km) north-east of Guisborough

Grid Ref: NZ 637193 (North York Moors Touring map)

The Miner's Experience

The Cleveland Ironstone industry flourished for just over a century until the last mine closed at North Skelton in 1964. Skinningrove was the place where the potential of the rich seams of Cleveland ironstone was discovered about 1850. Today you can relive the experiences of the men who mined the ironstone at the Tom Leonard Museum of Mining, which commemorates the local journalist who died in 1981 and has gathered together a collection of ironstone mining equipment and photographs. It is a developing museum and may be worth a number of visits over a few years.

As well as showing living conditions in the late nineteenth century, you go underground and pass the massive brick housing where a sirocco fan drew the foul air out of the mine. A level — a nearly horizontal tunnel which was used for drainage of water — leads into the hillside, where you experience how the men worked on the faces

in candle-lit conditions and what an explosion was like in these close confines. You also enter about a hundred yards into the tunnel where the ironstone was brought out. A visit to the museum will prove of interest to adults and children alike.

Site: in Skinningrove village just off the A174 Whitby to Saltburn road.

Grid Ref: NZ 712193 (North York Moors Touring map)

Andrew's Cow has Calved

In the late eighteenth and early nineteenth centuries the village of Saltburn was just an inn and sixteen houses. A remote place on the coast ideal for smuggling. John Andrews, the innkeeper in the early nineteenth century, was one of the most notorious smugglers along this stretch of coast and today there is a Smuggling Centre attached to the inn. When the cryptic message went round that Andrew's cow had calved, it meant that another load of smuggled goods had arrived.

Goods smuggled into the country ranged from gin and brandy to tea, playing cards, spinning wheels, continental cloth and copper kettles. All these were highly taxed and would show a good profit to the smugglers. Smuggling affected all levels of society, from the labourers who manhandled the goods from the boat to a safe haven, the shopkeepers who sold on the goods, to the gentry who often financed the whole operation. After serving one prison sentence for smuggling, John Andrews was captured a second time and, unable to pay the heavy fine, he died in prison eight years later.

Site: the Smuggling Centre is beside the Ship Inn, Old Saltburn, on the A174 Whitby to Saltburn road.

Grid Ref: NZ 670215 (Whitby, Landranger 94)

The Water-Powered Railway

When the new Victorian seaside resort of Saltburn was constructed on the cliff top, an easy way was required to take the visitors down to the sea and the pier. In July 1870 a vertical hoist was opened. The passengers went out on a narrow walkway, and as they approached the lift they were in a very exposed position with a 120 foot (36m) drop beyond the handrails. The wooden structure in which the cage operated was steadied by guy ropes. Up to twenty passengers could be raised at once, powered by water being transferred into a tank to counterbalance the weight of the passengers. After an inspection in 1883 the lift was dismantled, and the following year the present inclined tramway was opened. Like the hoist the tramway is powered by water pumped up to the top car; when it is heavier than the bottom car the brake is released and the ride begins.

Site: Saltburn is six miles (10km) north-east of Guisborough.

Grid Ref: NZ 666216 (Whitby, Landranger 94)

Ups and Downs of a Country House

Ormesby Hall is situated on the outskirts of Middlesbrough, but as you drive across the fields you could be miles from any urban environment. The house was built in the 1740s for James Pennyman, but he died before it was completed and his widow Dorothy supervised the final construction and fitting out of the house. The sixth baronet who took over the estate in 1770 was known as 'wicked Sir James' and he was interested in gambling and horse-racing. Eventually, deep in debt in 1781 he sold his Beverley town house and in 1789 he sold half of the estate and Ormesby.

In the 1850s the estate passed to the Worsley branch of the family and the estate prospered. It was bequeathed to the National Trust in 1961. Today visitors can tour the furnished house and see the kitchens and laundry, reminders of life both upstairs and downstairs.

Site: off the B1380 west of Ormesby, three miles (5km) south-east of Middlesbrough centre.

Grid Ref: NZ 529167 (North York Moors Touring map)

A Vanished Cottage

In 1755 Captain James Cook's father built a stone house in Great Ayton. That house now stands 12,000 miles away in Fitzroy Gardens, Melbourne, Australia. In 1933 the house came up for sale and it was bought by W Russell Grimwade. It was dismantled stone by stone and placed into 253 packing cases — even the creeper on the wall was packed! Everything was shipped to Melbourne and rebuilt there.

On the site of the cottage is now a garden with an obelisk of stones from Point Hicks Hill in Victoria — the first part of Australia to be sighted by Cook and his crew on the First Great Voyage of Exploration. To obtain the stone from this remote place, stone masons walked some twenty-six miles (42km) from the nearest settlement and spent several weeks cutting the stones and taking them to a nearby lighthouse. When the lighthouse was supplied with food and fuel, the stones were taken out and later shipped back to Great Ayton. Even these stones which form the obelisk have a history.

Site: in Great Ayton, about 100 yards (90m) along the road to Easby.

Grid Ref: NZ 557106 (North York Moors Touring map)

A Cleveland Treasure House

There was a plan some years ago to knock down Kirkleatham Old Hall, but thank goodness someone had the sense to preserve this treasure. The original Kirkleatham Hall was demolished and this building was the Free School. It was built for Sir William Turner between 1708 and 1709 by Cholmley. Set in fine gardens with free access, the building now houses a wealth of local bygones depicting life and work in the area. A walk round the displays and changing exhibitions will bring back memories to the older generation and questions from younger visitors.

Also available on the site are a picnic place, cafe and childrens' playground. The nearby Kirkleatham Owl Centre provides a fascinating look at birds of prey. Not only does the centre look after sick and injured birds but they also provide daily flying displays. As well as owls, there may be hawks and kites, and birds as large as vultures to be seen flying.

Site: signposted off the A174 Saltburn–Middlesbrough road, five miles (8km) west of Saltburn.

Grid Ref: NZ 593215 (Middlesbrough & Darlington, Landranger 93)

A Mini Matterhorn

The prominent hill of Roseberry Topping stands out from the moorlands to the east. When viewed from Newton under Roseberry it takes on the appearance of a mini Matterhorn. In an eighteenth century play it was said to be a mile and a half high — 7,920 feet (2,413m)! The sheer rocky summit is the result of ironstone mining. In 1914 the southern half of the hill collapsed onto the mine. The summit has been used for warning beacons and a celebration bonfire was lit there for Edward VII's coronation.

The shortest route to reach the top is from Newton under Roseberry where there is a car park. The climb can be made easier by circling the hill to ascend from the opposite side. From the top there are extensive views over the Cleveland Plain and across to the Pennines on the skyline; parts of Durham can be seen and an extensive area of the North Sea.

Site: Newton under Roseberry is on the A173 Stokesley to Guisborough road.

Grid Ref: NZ 579126 (North York Moors Touring Map)

Memorial to a Master Navigator

Standing 1,000 feet (300m) above sea level on Easby Moor, overlooking Great Ayton, is a fifty-one feet (15m) high stone monument. It was erected by local landowner, Robert Campion, in 1827 and commemorates Captain James Cook. From the hill top you can look over the Cleveland Plain to Marton where James Cook was born, and down to Airy Holme Farm, below Rose-berry Topping, where he spent his childhood. Rose-berry Topping itself is visible from the top of Easby Moor.

The foundation stone of the monument was laid on the 12th July 1827, the same day in 1776 that Captain Cook set sail from Plymouth on his third Great Voyage of Exploration. On the 27th October 1827 a crowd assembled to watch the top stone being placed in position on the centenary of his birth. The monument is visible from the North Sea where James Cook served his apprenticeship as a seaman.

The easiest approach to the monument is from the small car park at Gribdale Gate. A ten minute climb along a broad track leads to the monument on the heather-covered summit.

Site: from Great Ayton, follow the minor road past the railway station to a cattle grid at Gribdale Gate (NZ 592110).

Grid Ref: monument is at NZ 590101 (North York Moors Touring map)

The Cleveland Hills

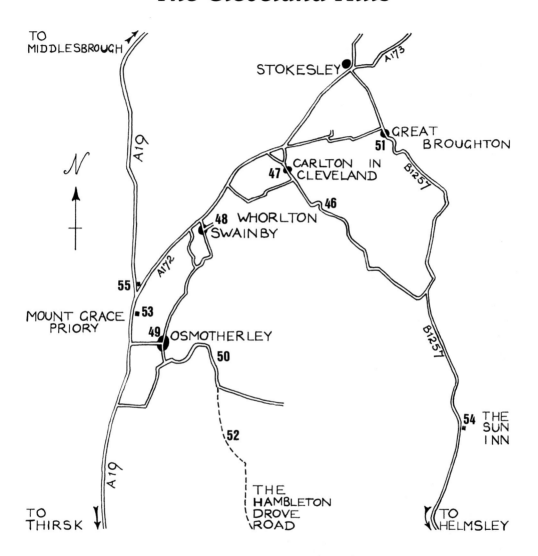

46 Lords's Stone cafe
47 Fox and Hounds,
   Carlton in Cleveland
48 Vanished village of Whorlton
49 Viewpoint, Rueberry Lane
50 Former Chequers Inn

51 Jet Miners Arms, Great Broughton
52 Hambleton Drove Road
53 Mount Grace Priory
54 Bobby Dawson's grave, Bilsdale
55 Cleveland Tontine Inn

An Underground Cafe

Just south of the col between Cringle Moor and Carlton Bank in the Cleveland Hills is the Three Lord's Stone. It marks the point where three lords' boundaries met. They were the estates of the Duncombe family of Helmsley, Marwood of Busby Hall, and Ailesbury who owned Snilesworth. Near the stone today stands a cafe built into the hillside in the early 1990s so as not to spoil the look of this remote area. Not only a popular place for a snack or a meal, it also obtains trade from walkers on the Cleveland Way and Lyke Wake Walk.

The road climbs steeply from Carlton village and at one time it was used for hill climbs to test vehicles. For modern cars it is no problem. There is a good view from the top of the hill looking over the Cleveland Plain to Middlesbrough, but a climb to the top of Cringle Moor to the east, using the Cleveland Way path, offers a more extensive panorama.

Site: three miles (5km) south of Stokesley on the minor road from Carlton in Cleveland to Chop Gate in Bilsdale.

Grid Ref: NZ 522030 (North York Moors Touring map)

The Parson Publican

When the Fox and Hounds Inn at Carlton in Cleveland came up for sale early this century, it was bought by the village vicar, Canon J L Kyle. The picturesque village three miles (5km) south of Stokesley had become a tourist attraction for the people from Teesside on Sundays. To stop the drunken brawling he changed the inn to a six-day licence, and also added tea and meals to the inn's tariff.

Canon Kyle was a remarkable man. He became the village vicar when it had no church. The former church, newly built, was gutted by fire in 1881 in strange circumstances and had never been rebuilt. Canon Kyle quickly set about gathering funds for the present church, and later to add the tower and pay for a new peal of bells. As well as being vicar and publican, he was a farmer noted for his black-faced sheep.

Site: the village is signposted off the A172 Stokesley to Thirsk road.

Grid Ref: NZ 507046 (North York Moors Touring map)

Another Vanished Village

Standing on a hillside overlooking the Cleveland Plain are the extensive remains of Whorlton Castle's fourteenth century gatehouse, built by Philip D'Arcy and Elizabeth Gray. Not far away in a less exposed position is the church of the Holy Cross. The village that the castle protected and the church served no longer exists. Has it drifted down over the centuries to form Swainby, standing beside Scugdale Beck?

Whorlton is mentioned in the *Domesday Book*. Swainby is first mentioned about 1300. It was probably in the late fifteenth and early sixteenth centuries that the population began to move down to a less exposed position in Swainby. Its growth may be due to the nearby drove road, and consequently drovers needing accommodation and somewhere to impound their cattle overnight. The village expanded in the nineteenth century when ironstone was discovered in Scugdale.

Site: Swainby is signposted of the A172 Stokesley to Thirsk road. Whorlton is reached by a cul-de-sac road near the church.

Grid Ref: NZ 481024 (North York Moors Touring map)

A Moorland Viewpoint

The village of Osmotherley stands on the edge of the moorlands overlooking the Vale of York. In the centre of the village is the market cross and close by is a stone table where farmers' wives sold spare produce. At the northern edge of the village is Rueberry Lane, used by walkers on the Cleveland Way.

A half-mile walk brings you to a fork in the tracks where there is an indicator pointing out the places of interest. It was erected in 1980 as a tribute to Walter Evans and points out the directions of Harrogate, Ripon, Wensleydale and Swaledale. Three fields away is the bustling traffic on the A19, while here is peace and tranquillity. The right fork leads up to the Lady Chapel which is attached to a house. It was probably built in the sixteenth century and is the setting of a number of miracles. Another footpath beyond the indicator leads down to Mount Grace Priory (see page 53).

Site: on the outskirts of Osmotherley on the Swainby road.

Grid Ref: indicator SE 452977; Lady Chapel SE 454981 (North York Moors Touring map)

A Former Cattle Drover's Inn

Standing in a remote position on Osmotherley Moor is Chequers Farm. Until recently it was an inn, and people walked there for a drink from as far away as Scotland. The road past the inn was used by the Scottish cattle drovers taking their animals south to be sold at the markets around London.

Arriving at the inn for the night, the cattle would be driven into stone wall enclosed fields to stop them straying overnight, and the drovers would eat, drink and spread the latest gossip they had picked up on their journey south. The inn's turf fire was one with a reputation for having burnt continuously for over a hundred years. Fastened to the wall of the farm is the original inn sign which states 'Be not in haste. Step in and taste. Ale to morrow for nothing', on the reasoning that tomorrow never came. Today the farm still caters to passing travellers with tea and cakes or soft drinks.

Site: on the minor road from Osmotherley to Hawnby, just over a mile (2km) from Osmotherley.

Grid Ref: SE 475970 (North York Moors Touring map)

Mining for Buried Treasure

Whitby is noted for its jet carving, an industry that boomed in Victorian times, and while some of the jet was picked up along the coast, much of the precious mineral was mined out of the Cleveland Hills.

It was a very speculative trade. The miner was looking for the fossilised remains of a tree buried and compressed millions of years ago. The jet was usually found around the 900 foot (270m) level high on the dale-sides. Today along the northern face of the Cleveland Hills and in Bilsdale you can see rows of spoil heaps.

The miner dug into the hillside and tipped the waste outside. If he was unsuccessful he moved on and dug into the hillside again. When a miner discovered jet, he took it down to one of the local inns on a prearranged date where agents from Whitby would be there to buy the jet. There is still a Jet Miners Arms in Great Broughton which opened about 1850 and a Jet Miners Track along the side of the Cleveland Hills.

Site: the Jet Miners Arms is on the B1257 Stokesley to Helmsley road in Great Broughton.

Grid Ref: NZ 547062 (North York Moors Touring map)

Beef on the Hoof

From the seventeenth to the middle of the nineteenth century, herds of hundreds of cattle were moved south from Scotland, on the hoof, to feed the growing population in the South of England, especially around London. After the Union with Scotland in 1707 it was estimated that the trade increased to over 30,000 Scottish cattle crossing the border each year. Many of these cattle came south along the Hambleton Drove Road, which climbed onto the moors near Swainby, past the Chequers Inn and over Black Hambleton to descend off the moors near Kilburn.

A drover may have had the entire wealth of four or five families entrusted to him. He had to get the cattle to market without them losing too much weight and avoiding the various cattle diseases. He also needed to know the route, avoiding toll roads and toll bridges which could be expensive. Having sold the cattle, he would walk back and distribute the money to the owners. He must be a man you could trust.

Site: the best stretch for walking is between the Osmotherley–Hawnby road at the foot of Black Hambleton and the top of Sneck Yat Bank.

Grid Refs: SE 479959 & SE 509877 (North York Moors Touring map)

Living like a Monk

Nestling under the western edge of the Cleveland Hills is the best-preserved Carthusian monastery in Britain. Whereas in most abbeys and priories the monks ate and worshipped together, in Mount Grace Priory they each inhabited a cell with its own small garden. Food was served to them in their cells and they were virtually self-contained. They passed the day in isolation and only rarely walked out into the cloisters that were enclosed by the cells. This order of monks had little contact with the local community.

The approach to the priory is through the former guesthouse, which later became a mansion. The most striking remains are of the church with the great cloister behind. One of the cells has been reconstructed as a Carthusian monk would have used it, so you can get a feel of the austere life in this priory.

Site: signposted off the A19, two miles (3km) north-west of Osmotherley.

Grid Ref: SE 448984 (North York Moors Touring map)

A Grave Dispute

Bobby Dowson was a respected member of the community in Bilsdale where he lived for over eighty years. As his gravestone records, he was the whip to the Bilsdale Hunt for upwards of sixty years and also wicket keeper for the Spout House cricket club for many years. When he died in 1902 his funeral was a noted local event.

The procession to the church was lead by the hearse driven by a member of the hunt, next came Bobby's pony carrying his whip, hunting coat, cap, boots and his spurs, the ex-master rode alongside the hounds and then the rest of the hunt followed. A collection was taken from the mourners for a suitable headstone to go over the grave. When it came to be erected the vicar refused his permission because of the fox's muzzle carving. After a long dispute the gravestone was placed outside the Sun Inn, where the hounds were kept and Bobby supped. It still stands there today.

Site: the Sun Inn is on the B1257 Stokesley to Helmsley road.

Grid Ref: SE 574935 (North York Moors Touring map)

Built by Tontine

The Cleveland Tontine Inn carries in its name the method by which it was created. With a potentially increasing number of stage coaches operating between Newcastle and Sunderland and York and London, there was a demand for a posting house where horses could be changed. In 1804, £2,500 was raised in £25 shares. All shareholders received a dividend until their death. When only three shareholders were left, the property became theirs in proportion to the number of shares each held.

The shares could be bought in anyone's name, but child mortality did not then mean that the youngest survived the longest. From the time of opening until the 1840s, when the railways eliminated the stage coaches, the inn served a wide variety of coaches. For some years it became a private house, but is now back serving the needs of passing travellers. The massive former stable block can still be seen behind the inn.

Site: at the junction of the A19 Thirsk–Middlesbrough road and the A172 to Stokesley.
Grid Ref: SE 443993 (North York Moors Touring map)

The Upper Esk Valley

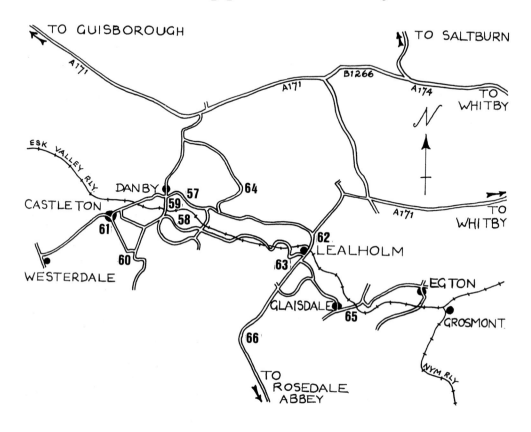

57 Moors Centre, Danby
58 Duck Bridge, Danby
59 Corn mill, Danby
60 Danby Church
61 Gallows Howe, Castleton
62 Memorial to two airmen,
    Lealholmside

63 Floodmarks, Lealholm, Esk Valley
64 Danby Beacon
65 Beggars Bridge, Glaisdale
66 Hart Leap, Glaisdale Rigg

The Moors Centre

This former hunting lodge nestling close to the infant River Esk is now a National Park Centre. There is free parking and free access to the centre. On display will be an exhibition on some aspect of the moor's flora and fauna or history. You can picnic in the grounds or use the tea rooms. For the more energetic you can walk along a nature trail, try your compass work around a marked-out course or follow a trail around the nearby countryside.

There are also a number of regular events which could include slide shows and talks in the lecture room, and guided walks with a theme visiting the sites of old local industries or some aspect of wildlife. There may be demonstrations of drystone walling, rug-making or quilting. This is *the* place to learn about many aspects of the North York Moors National Park.

Site: signposted off the A171 Whitby to Guisborough road, half a mile (1km) east of Danby village.

Grid Ref: NZ 715084 (North York Moors Touring map)

An Ancient Court

Spanning the River Esk not far from the National Park Centre at Danby Lodge is the ancient Duck Bridge, probably built in the latter part of the fourteenth century. It is named after George Duck who repaired the bridge in the eighteenth century. The steeply arched stone bridge is wide enough for walkers and packhorses, but the six foot three inch (190cm) width between the parapets was always a narrow squeeze in a car. The ford beside the bridge was originally for waggons and larger vehicles.

High on the hillside above the bridge is Danby Castle, the medieval home of the Latimers. This was where Catherine Parr, the last wife of Henry VIII, lived for a time. The castle buildings intermingle with a more modern farm, but one of the castle rooms is still used for the annual court leet of Danby. These court leets date back to medieval times when every manor had one. Now there are only thirty-eight in the country, of which four are on the North York Moors. They deal with encroachment and trespass on common land, and a jury of twelve local men hear the cases. They can also issue licences for gathering spagnum moss.

Site: about a mile (1.5km) east of Danby village just off the road to Lealholm.

Grid Ref: Duck Bridge NZ 719077, Danby Castle NZ 717072 (North York Moors Touring map)

The Village Miller

Nearly every village at one time had its mill for grinding corn, powered by either water or wind, but now very few remain in working order. Standing beside the River Esk is Danby Mill, with three sets of stones for grinding. A narrow path leads down to the tree-

fringed river where you can see the undershot water-wheel and the weir which keeps the water up to a suitable level. The undershot method is when the stream is channelled under the mill wheel to push the paddles round, as opposed to the overshot, breastshot and pitchback methods which were more efficient and utilised the weight of the water to provide the power.

At times the machinery is started, and you can watch the process of milling from the corn being hoisted to the top floor and its controlled descent through the stones to arrive as flour on the ground floor, a process that has happened on this site for over 350 years. There is also a tea room in the mill, and if you wish to stay the night in a mill the owners will provide bed and breakfast. At least it is a different form of accommodation!

Site: Danby is signposted off the A171 Whitby–Guisborough road. Carry straight on at the village crossroads and the mill is on your right beside the River Esk.

Grid Ref: NZ 707083 (North York Moors Touring map)

A Lonely Church

Danby Church stands in an isolated position in the middle of the dale over one and a half miles (2.5km) from the centre of Danby village. It is in fact nearer Castleton than Danby village.

Was there once a village near the church, or was the church built in Norman times so that it was central for all the farms in the dale?

The best-known incumbent of this lonely church was Rev J C Atkinson who is buried in the churchyard. He came to this remote moorland village in 1847 and stayed here until his death in 1900. During that time he studied the rich folklore of the area, dug into prehistoric barrows, recorded the local customs, and facts about the local weather and birdlife. All his studies came together in his book *Forty Years in a Moorland Parish* which was first published in 1891 and has since become a classic. This was still the time when folk tales about hobs, fairies, witches and wise men were related on winter evenings around a smouldering peat fire.

Site: from Danby village, on a minor road between Great Ayton and Egton Bridge, follow the signs to Danby Botton.

Grid Ref: NZ 696063 (North York Moors Touring map)

Gallows Howe

The expression 'better to be hanged for a sheep as a lamb' dates back to the times when there were numerous of-fences for which you could be hanged. Steal-ing either a lamb or a sheep was a capital offence so you may as well steal a sheep. It would provide more food for your family. In those hard times, the choice facing many people was to steal food to feed the family and risk being hanged, or allow everyone to starve to death.

Most towns and vil-lages over the centuries had gallows, usually beside the road to act as a deterrent to would-be wrongdoers. Castle-ton near the head of the Esk Valley still has the site of its gallows marked. Set just off the moorland road to Hut-ton le Hole is a large square stone pillar inscribed 'Gallows How 1835'. Who the last felon to be hanged at this place is not known, but surely it persuaded many people to be law-abiding.

Site: 100 yards (90m) west of the Castleton–Hutton le Hole road; 400 yards (360m) south of the Castleton boundary.

Grid Ref: NZ 681075 (North York Moors Touring map)

Two Heroes

Standing by the roadside at the entrance to the hamlet of Lealholmside is a memorial to two airmen. It commemorates Major Donald Schuyler and Lt Thomas Wheeler, both of the United States Air Force. They were in a United States Air Force F4C Phantom on a flight from RAF Alconbury in Huntingdonshire on the 27th April 1979. Flying some 300 feet (90m) above the valley floor the engine stalled, the pilot boosted the power and flames shot out of the rear of the aircraft. The crew stayed with the stricken aircraft and guided it across the fields just below the houses in Lealholmside and above the village of Lealholm.

The schoolchildren attending the village school heard a roar, then saw the blazing aircraft fly past. The pilot was seen to steer the aircraft away from the houses as it careered through a number of stone walls. Within days the villagers were searching for a suitable stone for a memorial to the two crewmen who lost their lives while saving the village.

Site: four miles (6.5km) east of Danby. The memorial is at the entrance to Lealholmside, half a mile (1km) north of Lealholm.

Grid Ref: NZ 766080 (North York Moors Touring map)

Esk Valley Floods

Near the side door of the Methodist church in Lealholm are two floodmarks indicating the height reached by the water in the River Esk. One is from the flood of 1840, a year after the church opened, and the higher of the two marks records the flood in 1930. A walk down the path beside the church leads to a set of stepping stones over the river, and you can imagine the depth of water and power of the flood at these times.

During the 1930 flood, the Lealholm miller and his son moved up to the second floor of the mill and took tools to cut through the ceiling to the third floor if necessary. Further downstream, the floodwater swept away bridges at Egton Bridge and Sleights. At Ruswarp a fishing coble manned by lifeboatmen was used to rescue two families who were trapped by the floods, including one family who were taken into the boat from their upstairs windows.

Site: on the Danby road out of Lealholm, ten miles (16km) west of Whitby.

Grid Ref: NZ 761075 (North York Moors Touring map)

The Sentinels

In Napoleonic times, a soldier kept watch at Danby Beacon waiting for the beacon signal that the French had invaded Britain. He was then to light his beacon and alert our forces inland. In this remote and lonely moorland place the soldier was allowed some comforts — a stone-built hut to protect him from the elements, and the company of his wife. Local men also had to assist in the round-the-clock vigil.

At the outbreak of the Second World War, Danby Beacon was ready to undertake the same role again. A radar station had been built a few hundred yards to the west. Today the site is marked by a plaque. They were part of a Chain Home (CH) system covering all of Britain, and aircraft could be detected eighty miles (130km) away.

DANBY BEACON
Site of
RAF RADAR STATION
1939 - 1954
THE MOUND BEHIND THIS MARKER
HOUSED THE EQUIPMENT WHICH
DETECTED AND LED TO THE
SHOOTING DOWN BY
FLT LIEUT. PETER TOWNSEND
OF THE FIRST ENEMY AIRCRAFT
TO FALL ON ENGLAND
3rd FEBRUARY 1940

The Heinkel shot down by Fl Lt Peter Townsend (see page 33) was identified sixty miles (96km) out to sea. The radar station was visited in November 1939 by King George VI and Robert Watson Watt who devised the system.

Site: two miles (3km) north-east of Danby village.
Turn off the A171 Whitby–Guisborough road and take the first turn left to Danby Beacon. The radar station site is just west of Danby Beacon.
Grid Ref: NZ 732096 (North York Moors Touring map)

The Lover's Bridge

Tom Ferris was the son of an Egton farmer in the late sixteenth century. He was courting Agnes Richardson, the squire's daughter at Glaisdale, but the match was not approved because of Tom's lower status. They met in secret whenever they could, but Tom realised that to win Agnes he would have to better himself. He obtained a position on a ship sailing out of Whitby to join the fleet being assembled against the Spanish Armada. On his last night before sailing, he went to see Agnes and found that he couldn't cross the flooded river between the villages. He vowed to build a bridge if he became rich so no other people would be parted by the river.

His voyage was a prosperous one and others followed. He eventually married Agnes and later became Lord Mayor of Hull. In 1619 he paid for the building of the steeply-arched stone Beggars Bridge, recalling Tom and Agnes's thwarted tryst in earlier days.

Site: eight miles (13km) south-west of Whitby beside the Egton–Glaisdale road.

Grid Ref: NZ 784054 (North York Moors Touring map)

Hart Leap

Standing on Glaisdale Rigg, between Great Fryup Dale and Glaisdale, are two small stone posts; one carries the inscription 'Hart Leap'. These two stones have stood there for many years and date back to medieval times when deer were hunted over these moors.

This particular deer was running northwards down the ridge pursued by the hunters and their dogs. At this point the terrified animal gave a tremendous leap over marshy ground.

The sight of this tremendous leap of 40 feet 6 inches (12.5m) astounded the hunters, who stopped and marked the places with sticks where the animal had launched itself on its tremendous leap and where it had landed. They probably feared that no one would believe them or that later the distance would become exaggerated. It is not known if the deer's leap for life succeeded, but let us hope it escaped while the huntsmen busied themselves marking the site.

Site: just over three miles (5km) south-west of Lealholm on the Rosedale Abbey road. At two footpath and two bridleway signs, walk thirty yards (10m) east onto the moor. Grid Ref: NZ 734035 (North York Moors Touring map)

The Hambleton Hills

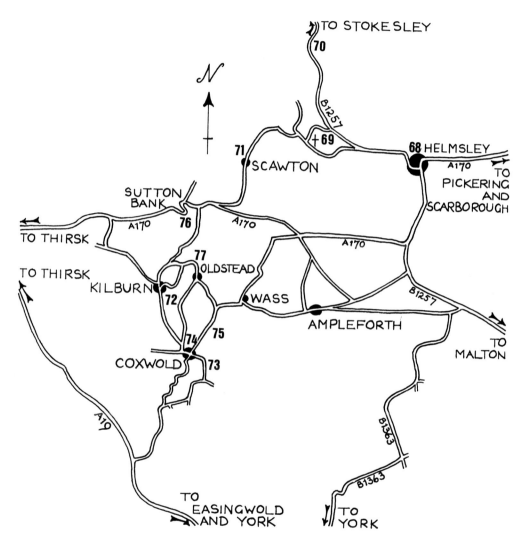

68 Helmsley Castle
69 Rievaulx Terrace
70 'Surprise view', Newgate Bank
71 Plaque to WWII airmen, Scawton
72 Robert Thompson's museum,
    Kilburn

73 Newburgh Priory
74 Shandy Hall, Coxwold
75 Byland Abbey
76 Sutton Bank and White Horse
77 Memorial chapel and site of
    Battle of Byland

The Victorious Defeat

On the 22nd November 1644 Colonel Jordan Crosland, the governor of Helmsley Castle, rode out of the castle followed by his 200 officers and men. They had with them their arms and goods. The soldiers were all armed, their weapons loaded and matches to ignite the weapons were lit. Their drums were beating and colours flying as the marched through the town, and were escorted to Scarborough Castle. What seems at first glance

to be a celebration was in fact the surrender of the castle by the Royalists to the Parliamentary forces.

A three month siege led by Sir Thomas Fairfax, in which he nearly lost his life in a skirmish, was over. Colonel Crosland had negotiated honourable terms for the surrender. The castle was then made unuseable by either side, but today you can walk around the ruins. The most impressive features are the massive embankments and ditches. One half of the lofty keep still stands, along with dwelling apartments and the curtain walls.

Site: town centre, Helmsley, which stands on the A170 Thirsk–Scarborough road.

Grid Ref: SE 610836 (North York Moors Touring map)

A Splendid Terrace

Standing above the ruins of Rievaulx Abbey (left) is Rievaulx Terrace, now in the care of the National Trust. The landscaping feature was built in the middle of the eighteenth century for Thomas Duncombe, who owned Duncombe Park near Helmsley. On the edge of a well-wooded escarpment is a half mile (0.8km) long grass terrace which passes between two landscaping 'temples', offering a number of wonderful views of the Rievaulx Abbey ruins.

The larger square-shaped 'temple' nearest the entrance has been used for banquets, and a table is prepared ready for just such an event. Below the dining room were the kitchens and caretaker's quarters (these are now used for an exhibition). The ceiling was painted by Bernici, a task he accomplished while suspended in slings. At the other end of the long terrace is a round 'Tuscan temple' (above). There is a similar length terrace in the grounds of Duncombe Park overlooking the River Rye.

Site: on the B1257, two miles (3km) north-west of Helmsley.

Grid Ref: entrance SE 582852 (North York Moors Touring map)

The 'Surprise View'

As the motorist drives north from Helmsley, the ground rises steadily until it reaches the top of Newgate Bank. At this point there is a 'surprise view' looking down the full length of Bilsdale. There is convenient parking beside the road and in the woods to the east. A path leads from the woodland car park to a stone observation platform. Here you can look over to the twin hills of Easterside and Hawnby Hill to the north-west.

The seemingly land-locked valley of Bilsdale has grass fields in the valley bottom, climbing to rough pasture, then heather and bracken; while at the head of the valley are the Cleveland Hills, with Botton Head, the highest point on the North York Moors, at 1,490 feet (454m). Newgate Bank Top was a beacon point during Napoleonic times, and took its warning light from beacons on the west side of Bilsdale and passed it on to Ampleforth Beacon further south.

Site: on the B1257 four and a half miles (7.25km) north-west of Helmsley.

Grid Ref: SE 563890 (North York Moors Touring map)

An Aircraft Tragedy

During the Second World War, the skies over the North York Moors were regularly scanned as the uneven beat of an aircraft engine was heard. Many aircraft returning from missions in occupied Europe had to clear the high ground of the North York Moors to reach their bases in the Vale of York. Many aircraft didn't make it with a tired crew and damage from anti-aircraft fire.

In March 1945 a Halifax bomber, crewed by members of the Free French Air Force, crashed near the village of Scawton. It was a cold and stormy night as the aircraft made its way back to its base. The pilot failed to clear the Hambleton Hills and the aircraft crashed into a tree, the crew bailing out at a low altitude. Three members of the crew survived. A plaque was placed on the tree at the crash site, and it was later moved to the church porch in Scawton, where it can still be seen recording the names of those who lost their lives.

Site: four miles (6.5km) west of Helmsley, signposted off the A170 Helmsley–Thirsk road.

Grid Ref: SE 549835 (North York Moors Touring map)

The Kilburn Mouseman

Recently, when an American furniture-maker decided to fit out the church at Monroe in Michigan as a memorial to his wife, he didn't turn to his own workshops but to Robert Thompson's workshops in Kilburn — he wanted the best.

In 1919 the village priest at Ampleforth wanted at large crucifix for the cemetery, and he was advised to get in touch with Robert Thompson who loved working in oak. From this commission Thompson received others for Ampleforth Abbey and School, and Gilling Castle. Each piece has a mouse carved into it as a trademark. As his fame grew, other churches required altar rails, pews and pulpits, and people wanted his sturdy furniture. Now his work can be seen in various parts of the world.

The story of the mouse trademark reputedly dates from a time early in Thompson's career when, while working in a church, his colleague remarked that they were 'as poor as church mice'. Thompson thought this would make an attractive emblem, and found himself carving a mouse on whatever he was working on at the time

Around the village of Kilburn you can see stacks of oak maturing, and opposite the half-timbered showroom is the Carver's Museum where you can see various pieces of work that have been produced in the workshops and craftsmen working on the latest orders.

Site: Seven miles (11km) south-west of Helmsley, best reached by Ampleforth and Coxwold.

Grid Ref: SE 513796 (North York Moors Touring map)

Oliver Cromwell's Burial Place?

Newburgh Priory, set on the outskirts of the picturesque village of Coxwold, was built for the Augustinian canons in 1145. At the Dissolution of the Monasteries in 1538 the estate passed to the Belasyse family, who converted the building to a private house. The house and grounds, which include fine rock and water gardens, are now open at certain times to the public.

During the Commonwealth period, Oliver Cromwell's daughter Mary married into the family. Tradition states that, at the restoration of the monarchy, Mary brought her father's body to Newburgh Priory and substituted another body in the grave. It was this other corpse that was exhumed, hung at Tyburn and later interred in Westminster Abbey. Do Oliver Cromwell's remains lie in the room which bears his name in Newburgh Priory?

In the latter part of the nineteenth century Edward VII, while Prince of Wales, visited the house and asked for the tomb to be opened. As a compromise a hole was drilled in one of the planks, but nothing was proved.

Site: seven miles (11km) south-west of Helmsley; half a mile (1km) south of Coxwold.

Grid Ref: SE 543764 (North York Moors Touring map)

A Literary Shrine

On the western edge of Coxwold village stands Shandy Hall, an unusual old house whose predominant features seem to be gables and chimneys. It was built about 1450 as a timber-framed house centred on a large hall, and was later divided up into more practical rooms. In 1760 it became the home of Laurence Sterne for the last eight years of his life. He had come to the village as the parson, but he was equally at home in the literary circles of London. That same year had seen the publication of the first two parts of his masterly comic novel *Tristram Shandy*, which had seen him fêted by London society and ensured his subsequent reputation as the forerunner of the modern novel.

In this quaint house he finished *Tristam Shandy* — which is where the house gets its name — and also wrote *A Sentimental Journey*. His study contains a library of his works and other books he may have used. Laurence Sterne died in London in 1768 and was buried there. When St George's burial ground in Bayswater Road was cleared in 1969, his remains were brought back to Coxwold and re-interred across the road in the church where he had preached to the villagers.

Site: seven miles (11km) south-west of Helmsley.

Grid Ref: SE 531772 (North York Moors Touring map)

The Search for Byland Abbey

Byland Abbey stands beneath the wooded heights of the Hambleton Hills, but it took four attempts to arrive at this site. About 1138, Abbot Gerald and twelve monks left Furness Abbey in Cumbria and travelled east, establishing a monastic house on land at Hood, north-west of Kilburn. This site proved too small, and five years later they moved to a site near Old Byland, four miles west of Helmsley.

The sound of the bells that called the monks to prayer were often confused with the bells at Rievaulx Abbey only a mile and a half (2km) away. In 1147 they moved again to Stocking, a third site provided by Roger de Mowbray, about a mile to the south. In 1177 they moved to the present site at Byland and created the magnificent abbey

whose remains you can see today. This site is now in the care of English Heritage. Looking at the extensive ruins today, you can mentally recreate the life of a medieval monk.

Site: five miles (8km) south-west of Helmsley on the road from Ampleforth to Coxwold.

Grid Ref: SE 549789 (North York Moors Tourist Map)

A Climb to the Moors

The road from Thirsk to Helmsley climbs steeply onto the Hambleton Hills at Sutton Bank. The mile-long climb is 1 in 4 (25%) now, but in the 1920s the hill was poorly engineered and graded, so it was used for hill climbs, with only the best cars reaching the top. From the plateau top there is an extensive view across the Vale of York to the Yorkshire Dales.

This is a popular wayside stop for motorists, and there is an information centre situated near the car park. A short walk over the road leads to a view indicator pointing out the many places of interest which can be seen on a clear day. A scenic stroll to the south along the escarpment reveals Lake Gormire tucked into the foothills, and if you continue along the Cleveland Way for just over a mile (2km) it leads to the Kilburn White

Horse hill carving. A nature trail leads down to Lake Gormire from the information centre.

Site: on the A 170, seven miles (11km) west of Helmsley.

Grid Ref: SE 514829 (North York Moors Touring map)

A Battlefield Memorial

Tucked away on the side of the Hambleton Hills is a small stone chapel converted from a farm building. It was created in the 1950s by John Bunting as a memorial to three former schoolboys from Ampleforth College who died in the Second World War and another who died in Northern Ireland. The chapel is only open for special services, but you can admire the finely-carved doors and the surrounding scenery.

This area was the site of the Battle of Byland in 1322. Scots were pursuing English forces led by Edward II, who had been raiding over the border. The English forces, on the high ground, were in a good defensive position until they were outflanked at Scotch Corner. The Scots then turned the battle in their favour, and Edward II had to make a speedy flight on horseback to the safety of York.

Site: from the village of Oldstead, six miles (9.5km) south-west of Helmsley, walk along the road to Kilburn, turn right after Sand Lane House, then left at the Cockerdale Farm sign. A long climb leads through fine scenery to Scotch Corner.

Grid Ref: SE 526814 (North York Moors Touring map)

The Southern Dales

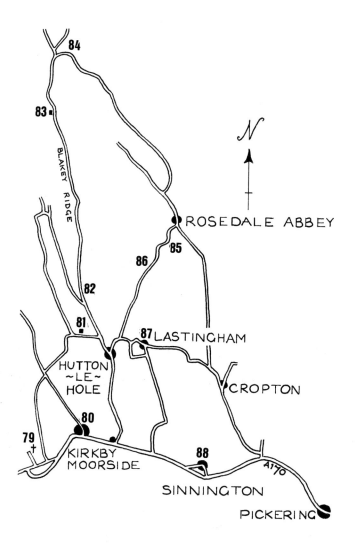

A Saxon Minster

Tucked away in a peaceful valley beside Hodge Beck is Kirkdale Minster. It is reached along a cul-de-sac road off the old Kirbymoorside to Helmsley road. It does not stand in the centre of a village because the community it has served for over 1,000 years lies scattered over many miles. The parish stretches from the moorland heights above Bransdale to the lush farmland around Muscoates, beside the River Rye, a distance of some sixteen miles (26km). In the Middle Ages, when church attendance was compulsory, the parishioners would arrive from Muscoates, North Holme, Welburn and Wombleton to the south, Nawton to the west, and Skiplam and Bransdale to the north.

The minster may have been established in the seventh century by St Aidan, along with Stonegrave Minster and Lastingham Church to act as centres from which monks could spread the gospel to the surrounding countryfolk. Under the porch of the church is a sundial recording that Orm rebuilt the church — and that was before the Norman Conquest in 1066!

Site: one and a half miles (2km) west of Kirkbymoorside, signposted off the A170.
Grid Ref: SE 857676 (North York Moors Touring map)

The Master Blacksmith

In the days when education was not widespread, trade signs were developed so that illiterate people could tell what wares were for sale at a particular shop. In Kirkbymoorside many people drive from the roundabout into the town without noticing Christopher Carter's trade sign. He was the eldest son of a blacksmith, and carried on his father's trade in the 1840s at the Ryedale Forge. He invented and built a portable threshing machine, manufactured bricks and tiles, and supplied Kirkbymoorside with gas.

When he wanted a new shopfront, he created it out of the material with which he was familiar. Two shopfronts and an archway entrance are made out of iron cast in his foundry. Incorporated into the frontage are the words Gas Works, Foundry and C' Carter for the benefit of his literate clientele.

Close by is Kirk Forge, which was operated by Wilfred Dowson from the 1940s to the 1960s and who became nationally known for his fine wrought ironwork.

Site: the east side of Railway Street, Kirkbymoorside, which is just off the A170 Pickering to Helmsley road.

Grid Ref: SE 697863 (North York Moors Touring map)

An Industrial Area?

Farndale is noted for its fine display of daffodils that spread a yellow carpet of colour along the banks of the River Dove each spring. Just upstream from the road bridge at Lowna in Farndale is a farm that from medieval times had a number of industrial uses. It was a fulling mill where woollen cloth was pounded by hammers operated by a water wheel turned by the River Dove. The action removed grease and oil from the wool, and compacted it into a stronger material.

Early in the nineteenth century it became a corn mill and later a tannery. The steeping pits where the hides were treated are still on site, and you can see the louvre-shuttered windows which allowed the air through to dry the leather. The mill machinery chopped up oak bark for the tanning process and also for crushing bones into fertiliser, which was a sideline. About 1915 the tannery closed, and it continued as a farm long before any authorities would want to monitor pollution levels in the river.

Site: three miles (5km) north of Kirkbymoorside on the Hutton le Hole to Gillamoor road.

Grid Ref: SE 687910 (North York Moors Tourist Map)

Moorland Signposts

As the motorist or walker crosses the moors today, it is relatively easy to find the way to any village or town with the help of detailed maps. Up to the early eighteenth century it was far more difficult and depended on local knowledge. Many travellers from outside the district hired guides. In mist or snow the few upright stones that acted as markers could prove difficult to find, and many travellers died on the moors. In the nineteenth century one body was only identified as a pedlar by the corks scattered around him — he had been visiting the isolated farms and inns selling the corks for stoppering bottles.

In 1711 it became law that guideposts were to be set up at every crossroads in the North Riding. These would indicate to travellers where the roads lead. There are still a number on the moors, and one of the finest examples is on Blakey Ridge, and indicates the roads to Pickering and Malton, Kirbymoorside and Guisbrough. The stonemason has marked round his hand and carved out the direction to travel!

Site: one and a half miles (2km) north of Hutton le Hole on the Castleton road.

Grid Ref: SE 693925 (North York Moors Touring map)

The Inn at Blakey

Standing 1,290 feet (400m) above sea level, on one of the highest parts of the North York Moors, is the Lion Inn at Blakey. It stands beside the unfenced moorland road which has probably been in use since prehistoric times. There are no locals now, the nearest communities being some 800 feet (240m) below in the valleys of Rosedale and Farndale. But about a hundred years ago the area was alive with people. A quarter of a mile (350m) down the road were the railway men and their families at Rosedale Junction, where the two spurs of the mineral railway met. Close by was a small iron mine set on the ridge, and there were moorland coal pits to the north.

Set above the inn is Cockpit Howe, a bronze age burial mound. As with many howes the centre part had collapsed, leaving a natural amphitheatre. This was used for the barbaric sport of cockfighting. The remote situation of the inn may have lead to its continued use after the 'sport' was made illegal.

Site: beside the Hutton le Hole to Castleton road, six and a half miles (10km) north of Hutton le Hole.

Grid Ref: SE 678997 (North York Moors Touring map)

Moorland Crosses

On the watershed of the moors above Rosedale are four moorland crosses. They were erected at various times between the twelfth and eighteenth centuries to act as waymarkers for travellers. Possibly some were erected at the expense of the abbeys. They would seem to indicate a track running along the high ridge of the moors.

The Lyke Wake Walk, devised by Bill Cowley in 1955, crosses the high moors for forty miles (64km), and the North York Moors Crosses Walk passes these crosses, but they were erected much earlier for travellers heading in a north–south direction.

Young Ralph Cross (right) is set beside the Castleton–Hutton le Hole road, which was used for transporting moorland

coal and lime before the railways arrived. Further westward on the moor is Old Ralph Cross, marking the route south from Guisborough Priory through Westerdale, and down into Ryedale and York. Fat Betty or White Cross (left), standing at the head of Rosedale, probably indicated a route between Rosedale and Westerdale. The socket stone and part of the shaft remain of Botton Cross, which marked the ridge road into Fryup Dale.

Sites: Fat Betty and Young Ralph Cross are beside the Rosedale Abbey to Westerdale road.

Grid Refs: Young Ralph SE 677021; Old Ralph SE 672020; Fat Betty SE 683020; Botton Cross SE 697020 (North York Moors Touring Map)

Rosedale Hill Climb

On the 1st May 1921 over 1,000 cars and motorcycles gathered in the rural solitude of Rosedale. The attraction that had brought the visitors was the 'freak' hill of Rosedale Chimney or Rosedale Abbey Bank. (The chimney itself is pictured right.) As car and motorcycle performances had improved, there grew a group of people who wanted to test their machines against the steepest roads possible. Rosedale Chimney offered sections as steep as 1 in 2.5 (40%).

The motorcycle event in 1921 was won by Arthur Champion of Rosedale on a 3.5 hp BSA. In 1923 the winning time for the ascent was 1 minute 17.8 seconds in a 30/98 Vauxhall, a time that would be difficult to beat today. Later it became a regular part of the annual endurance race 'Scoot to Scotland'. You can still try your driving skills on the steep hill today, but it is now well surfaced and better graded. It has featured recently in advertisements as the steepest hill in Britain.

Site: on the Rosedale Abbey–Hutton le Hole road.

Grid Ref: start SE 723952 (North York Moors Touring map)

Motor Hill Climb Ros[e]dale Abbey. June 1914.

Rosedale Ironstone

Standing some 600 feet (280m) above the picturesque village of Rosedale Abbey are some massive stone kilns. They were erected in the 1860s to reduce transport costs for the ironstone mining companies who extracted ore from the dale between 1860 and 1920. The first mine to begin operating in 1856 was near Hollins Farm on the west side of Rosedale. By 1861 the railway had been built to carry the ore northwards to the iron foundries.

The ore was hauled up an incline by a stationary engine. The fumes from the engine passed up the famous fifty foot (15m) high Rosedale Chimney, which was a landmark until it was pulled down in 1972. The chimney was built to stop the landowner's grouse being disturbed by the smoke. The ore was then tipped into the massive calcining kilns to burn off any waste products — after all, they were paying sixpence (2.5p) per ton for the ironstone.

Site: the easiest approach is from Hutton le Hole along the road to Rosedale Abbey. It is a steep climb from Rosedale Abbey up Rosedale Abbey Bank (see previous page).

Grid Ref: SE 720948 (North York Moors Touring map)

Saint Cedd's Church

Nestling under the brow of the Tabular Hills, with Spaunton Moor stretching away to the north, is the delightful village of Lastingham. This was where Saint Cedd established a monastery in AD 654. Some 200 years later a pillaging party of Danes destroyed the monastery. In 1078 Abbot Stephen of Whitby Abbey re-established the monastery and built a crypt as a shrine to Saint Cedd. Visitors to the church can still walk down the stairs into the crypt and view this unusual feature.

Opposite the church is the village inn. In the eighteenth century it was run by Rev Carter, who was brought before an ecclesiastical court for allowing disorderly conduct. He explained that he had difficulty keeping his wife and thirteen children on his stipend of £20. He provided food for his family by fishing in local streams and his wife ran the inn. He explained that he only played the fiddle at the inn to stop customers from quarrelling. The court accepted his explanation!

Site: three miles (5km) north-west of Kirkbymoorside.

Grid Ref: SE 727904 (North York Moors Touring map)

Picturesque Sinnington

The stone houses of Sinnington stand around the spacious village green. The most notable feature is the lofty maypole, which has been replaced on each occasion it has fallen. Close by on the village green is a small bridge with no stream beneath. The reason for its construction is now lost. It may have crossed a mill leet drawing water from the river to power a mill wheel further downstream, as there is evidence of a medieval mill but its site is not known. It may only have been a crossing point over a flood channel for pedestrians and horsemen, with a ford close by for waggons.

The bridge is in line with the original road towards Pickering, which headed north-eastwards out of the village past the interesting church. If you look around the stonework which forms the wall of the church, you can see parts of a broken Saxon cross that have been used in its construction. Close by, at Hall Farm, is a large stone barn that was the twelfth century great hall of the Barons de Clere.

Site: three miles (5km) east of Kirkbymoorside, signposted off the A170.

Grid Ref: SE 744858 (North York Moors Touring map)

Gateway to the Moors

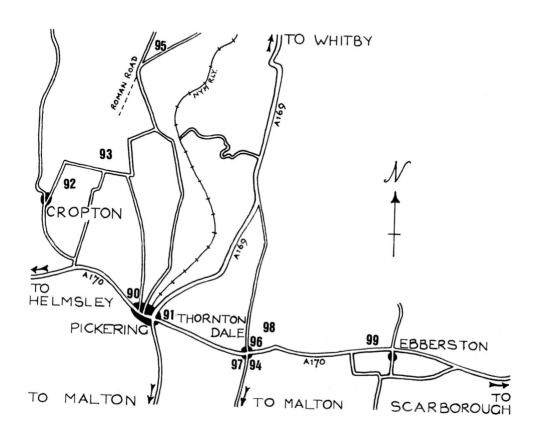

90 Beck Isle Museum, Pickering
91 Pickering Castle
92 Memorial seats, Cropton
93 Cawthorn Camps
94 Hooping iron, Thornton Dale

95 Mauley Cross, Cropton Forest
96 Matthew Grimes's grave,
    Thornton Dale
97 Village stocks, Thornton Dale
98 Ellerburn village
99 Ebberston Hall

A Treasure House

Standing beside Pickering Beck is the large stone building which houses the Beck Isle Museum. The building, its yard and outhouses are crammed with many family treasures. Those souvenirs of a time long gone; reminders of a craftsman's trade, or the goods a family sold from their shop for many years. All are on display to recall memories or enlighten youngsters on how they were used.

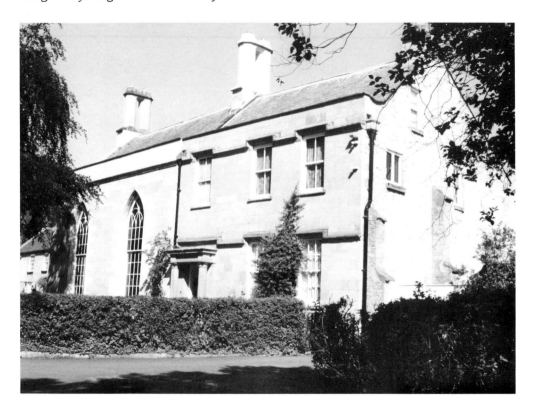

There are twenty-seven display areas, including an old printing machine that is still in use. There is also a room full of cameras, some of which were used by Sidney Smith, a local photographer who captured both local events, and the changing patterns of light and shade that enhanced his pictorial photographs — many of his prints are on display around the museum. The house was originally the home of William Marshall, a noted agriculturalist of the late eighteenth century.

Site: Bridge Street, Pickering, 100 yards (90m) west of the railway station.

Grid Ref: SE 796841 (North York Moors Touring map)

The Royal Castle

Pickering Castle, now in the care of English Heritage, stands on high ground to the north of the town overlooking Pickering Beck

The first castle was built late in the eleventh century. The formidable curtain walls still stand, and in the grounds is the motte with the remains of the keep. More of this royal castle would still have been left standing if it had not been for the people who were supposed to be protecting the sovereign's interest. In 1495, Sir Richard Cholmley held all four senior positions in the honor of Pickering: he was receiver, appointed to receive all monies; seneschal, who administered justice and was responsible for controlling the domestic affairs of the castle; constable; and master forester.

The titles and privileges passed down the family, and in the middle of the sixteenth century Sir Richard Cholmley was charged with sending two masons into the castle to pull down the Kings Hall and the tower and stairs, removing fourteen wagonloads of stone and two wagonload of slates to improve his own home at Roxby Castle, just to the west of Thornton Dale. Paradoxically, Roxby Castle no longer exists.

Site: at the end of Castlegate in Pickering.

Grid Ref: SE 798845 (North York Moors Touring map)

Memorial Seats

War memorials to those people who gave their lives in two world wars have taken many forms. The village of Cropton, standing on the southern edge of the North York Moors, have commemorated their fallen in a very practical way. Placed around the village, often at local viewpoints, are memorial seats with the name of the person commemorated inscribed on the seat back.

In the triangle of roads to the west of the village (SE 756890), under the chestnut tree, is the metal seat to Eric Pierson, who died on the 8th September 1944. Halfway down the hill leading to Rosedale Abbey (SE 752892) is a seat to Jim Flintoft, who died on the 15th May 1941. At the bends on the east side of the village (SE 759896) is the seat to Fred Dawson, who died on the 29th September 1940; and a mile (1.5km) further along the road, at the junction to Sutherland (SE 770894), is a seat (pictured) to James S Cameron, who died on the 18th February 1945. All are very practical memorials in this scenic area, where a rest during a walk gives much pleasure.

Site: Cropton lies two miles (3.25km) north of the Pickering to Kirkbymoorside road.

Grid Refs: as quoted (North York Moors Touring map)

Cawthorn Camps

Standing on the edge of the Tabular Hills, with fine views to the north, are the Cawthorn Camps. From a pleasant car park set in a wood, a scenic path leads northwards to the large earthworks constructed by the Romans to defend their camps. Why the camps were built is open to speculation. They stand beside the Roman road (see page 109) from Malton to Lease Rigg above Grosmont. The camps may have been garrisoned to show local people the Roman presence in the area, to house the people building the road or for soldiers on manoeuvres.

The site was excavated by Professor Richmond between 1923 and 1929, and his conclusions were that the site had been occupied twice for a short time, possibly as little as six to ten years apart. It seems probable that the camps were constructed between AD 80 and 120. While it may have been a poor posting for Roman soldiers, today it offers an interesting walk with fine views.

Site: Signposted off the Newton on Rawcliffe to Cropton road four miles (6.5km) north of Pickering.

Grid Ref: SE 784901 (North York Moors Touring map)

Changing a Tyre

While changing a tyre for today's motorist is a relatively simple operation, in the days of horse and carts it required a blacksmith. Standing by the stream in Thornton Dale is the old blacksmith's forge (now the Forge gift shop) and fastened to the wall is a hooping iron, the iron band

that formed the tyre around the wooden wheel. This was placed in the cramp and slowly fed through the jig as a downward pressure was exerted. This action curved the tyre to the rough shape of the wheel. When the tyre had been made, it was heated up and placed over the wheel. The wheel and tyre were then thrown into the stream, and the tyre rapidly contracted onto the wood in the cold water. Most blacksmiths had to pour water onto the tyre, but the convenient stream made life easier for the Thornton Dale blacksmith.

Site: near the crossroads in Thornton Dale, two miles (3.25km) east of Pickering.

Grid Ref: SE 834830 (North York Moors Touring map)

A Lost Moorland Road

Standing beside a hard-core road through Cropton Forest is Mauley Cross, named after a medieval landowner, Peter de Mauley. This is one of five complete medieval crosses on the North York Moors.

As late as the middle of the eighteenth century, people crossing the moors between Malton and Whitby were recommended to hire a local guide. A road south from Whitby to Pickering and Kirkbymoorside passed Mauley Cross. When the toll road following the route of the present Pickering–Whitby road was opened, this moorland road increased in popularity with thrifty Yorkshiremen as no tolls were payable.

Eventually, though, the route did decline and is now lost. The route from Sleights climbed to Sil Howe above Goathland, then descended to Abbots House and Thornhill, before climbing the side of Simon Howe. The track continued to Brown Howe Cross, before continuing south to either Pickering or Kirkbymoorside. Some of the last vehicles to use the road were wagons from Helmsley delivering oaks to Whitby shipyards in the early nineteenth century.

Site: just off the road from Newton on Rawcliffe to Egton Bridge six and a half miles (10km) north of Pickering.

Grid Ref: SE 796943 (North York Moors Touring map)

Napoleon's Pall Bearer

Walking through the picturesque village of Thornton Dale, you can imagine most of the local people did not travel far before the coming of the railways. In the churchyard is the grave of Matthew Grimes, who was born in 1779 and he certainly did a great deal of travelling. On his gravestone is recorded the fact that, as a soldier in the 20th and 24th Infantry, he served in India and in the Peninsular War. He had also been present at Napoleon's final defeat at Waterloo.

He guarded Napoleon when he was exiled on St Helena in the South Atlantic, and on his death acted as pall bearer when the emperor was carried to his grave on the island. The stories of his adventures in many parts of the world would have provided hours of entertainment for the villagers in Thornton Dale.

Site: on the A170, two miles (3.25km) east of Pickering.

Grid Ref: SE 838831 (North York Moors Touring map)

Ancient Justice

Set near the crossroads in Thornton Dale is the market cross, and close by are the village stocks. The last occasion that the village's stocks were used was in 1874. People were placed in the stocks for minor offences, but it was still a harsh punishment. The offender was usually placed in the stocks on market day so everyone in the village was aware who had carried out the crime or misdemeanour.

As well as being exposed to the elements from dawn until dusk, the felon was also an easy target for anyone who wanted to get revenge. Often after the offender was released he was numb and unable to walk, and had to be assisted by friends. The village also possessed a small prison for detaining vagrants and thieves, known as the Black Hole. It was set beneath the Poor House, and the last woman detained in there about 1850 was released by four men who broke into the cell.

Site: near the crossroads on the A170, two miles (3.25km) east of Pickering.

Grid Ref: SE 834830 (North York Moors Touring map)

A Lost Valley of Industry

Standing a mile north of Thornton Dale is the peaceful hamlet of Ellerburn. It is easily reached from Thornton Dale by a pleasant walk over the fields or by way of the narrow cul-de-sac road.

Parts of the small, stone-built church date back to the eleventh century. If you pass through the lychgate and examine the church walls, you will discover pieces of stonework that have had other uses, including parts of a carved cross. Looking around, you would not suspect that this quiet hamlet once had a number of industries.

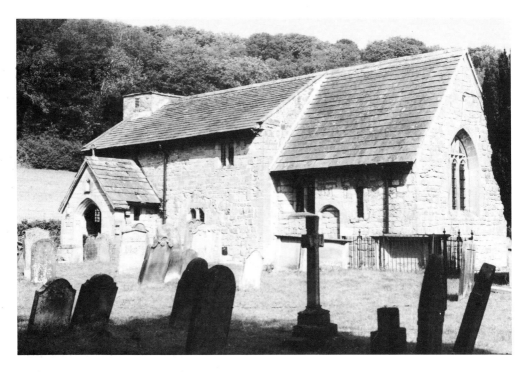

Opposite the church is Low Farm, which was once a medieval corn mill and was later used for fulling cloth and as a bleach mill. Further up the valley are High and Low Paper Mill Farms. These paper mills were in operation in the late seventeenth century and produced sheets of paper from linen rags. A walk along the streamside will hopefully reveal a dipper searching for food, which may be easier to see than Ellerburn's former industries.

Site: signposted off Whitbygate, Thornton Dale, three miles (4.5km) east of Pickering.
Grid Refs: church SE 841841; Low Paper Mill Farm SE 846841; High Paper Mill Farm SE 843851 (North York Moors Touring map)

Small is Beautiful

When you think of stately homes, you imagine massive houses set in hundreds of acres of parkland. One glance at Ebberston Hall, standing just off the Pickering to Scarborough road, reveals a different stately home.

A grand stone staircase leads up to the imposing front door of this Palladian mansion, but what you notice is its small size. The house has only eleven rooms. It was built in 1718 by Colen Campbell for William Thompson, MP for Scarborough and warden of the Mint. The rear loggia overlooked a water garden of pools and cascades which reappeared at the front of the house.

In 1814 the house became the home of George Osbaldeston, the most famous squire of his day. He was always short of money due to spending six days a week hunting, shooting, duelling, playing cricket and tennis, and gambling. He once rode 200 miles in ten hours to win a 1,000 guinea bet. He finally managed to marry a rich widow, who kept him in order and in the style to which he was accustomed.

Site: north of the A170 between Allerston and Ebberston, 5.5 miles (9km) east of Pickering.

Grid Ref: SE 892834 (North York Moors Touring map)

Heart of the Moors

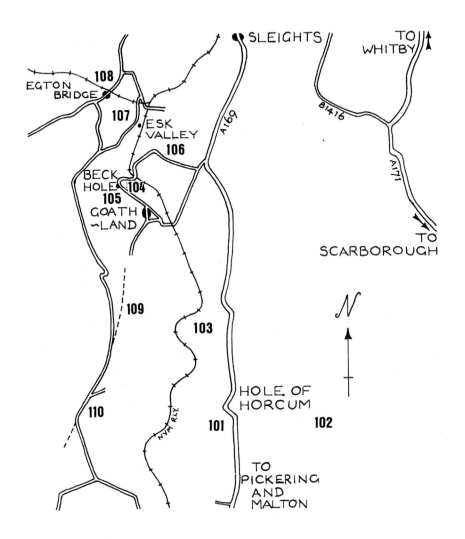

101 Hole of Horcum
102 Malo Cross, Saltergate Brow
103 North York Moors Railway,
    Fen Bog
104 Quoits at Beck Hole
105 Rope-hauled Railway, Beck Hole
    to Goathland

106 Whinstone outcrop, Sil Howe
107 Hamlet of Esk Valley
108 Postgate Inn, Egton Bridge
109 Roman Road near Egton Bridge
110 Old Wives' Well, Stape

The Giant's Hollow

Travellers crossing the moors from Pickering to Whitby pass around the vast hollow called the Hole of Horcum. Many years ago, children who asked who had made the hollow were told that it was the Giant Wade. He had scooped out the hollow and threw the earth at his wife Bell. The huge piece of moorland missed and Blakey Topping, a hill a mile to the east, was formed.

The Hole of Horcum has a large car park and is a popular place for tourists and walkers, while in recent years model aeroplanes and hang gliders have soared above the hollow.

The real reason for the hollow is perhaps even more incredible. Flowing southwards out of the hollow is tiny Levisham Beck. Over thousands of years, springs have washed away the lower soil and rocks, and the moorland above has collapsed into the hollow. All the moorland has been washed down the tiny stream. Up to a few years ago the hollow supported two farms at High and Low Horcum.

Site: beside the A169 Pickering–Whitby road seven miles (11km) north of Pickering.

Grid Ref: SE 853937 (North York Moors Touring map)

The Cross that Reappeared

From the car park beside the Hole of Horcum at the top of Saltergate Bank is an access road to Newgate Foot Farm. If you walk down the road and turn left at the end of the trees, the footpath leads onto Saltergate Brow, and there is a fine walk north east-wards with good views. The track eventually slants down the hillside to reach Malo Cross which, like Mauley Cross (see page 95), takes its name from Peter de Mauley, a medieval landowner.

Early this century the cross disappeared and it stood for a while in Doctor Kirk's garden in Pickering. He was an avid collector of bygone items, and his collection eventually became the basis of the Castle Museum in York. Did some local farmer with a doctor's bill to pay offer the cross in settlement? Many years later the cross was brought back from Pickering and re-erected on its original site.

Site: a mile (1.5km) to the east of the A169 Pickering–Whitby road at Saltergate Bank Top, eight miles (13km) north of Pickering.

Grid Ref: SE 866949 (North York Moors Touring map)

The Floating Railway

In the early nineteenth century, Whitby was cut off from the rest of Britain by the inhospitable moors. A scheme had been looked at to build a canal to Pickering, but it never reached fruition. In the 1830s Whitby businessmen looked towards the new railways for a link across the moors, and consulted George Stephenson. It was agreed to build a simple tramway operated by horse-drawn carriages.

During the construction special problems were encountered at Fen Bog, which was the summit of the railway. The moorland bog at this point was twenty feet (6m) deep. Large balks of timber were driven into the bog with massive hammers. Then sheaves of heather were wrapped in sheepskins and thrown into the bog, trees and hurdles were placed there, and eventually a firm enough raft was established to carry the railway. The rest of Fen Bog is now a small nature reserve, but the passengers on the North York Moors Railway still pass by unaware of the problems it caused.

Site: 200 yards (180m) west of the A169 Whitby–Pickering road at Eller Beck Bridge.
Grid Ref: SE853980 (North York Moors Touring map)

Quoits

On the green in the picturesque hamlet of Beck Hole are four wooden boxes covering the playing area of a game which has virtually disappeared in most parts of Britain. However, there is still a strong competitive league for the sport along the Esk Valley, and you may be lucky and see the game being played on an evening or a Saturday afternoon in summer.

The picture shows the game being played, though not at Beck Hole. The pitch is eleven yards (10m) long from a pin set in clay to another pin set in clay. The object of the game is to throw the quoit, a metal hoop which weighs 5¼lb (2.4kg), over the pin — a 'ringer'. But there are other moves in this game, such as a 'gater' which lands against the pin, preventing your opponent throwing a 'ringer'. Other throws may be termed a 'pot', 'quew' or 'Frenchman'.

There are few better ways to spend a sunny afternoon than by watching the game being played. You may come away with some added knowledge of this ancient game — or be even more puzzled than when you arrived.

Site: Beck Hole is a mile (1.5km) north-west of Goathland and reached by steep hills.

Grid Ref: NZ 821022 (North York Moors Touring map)

The Rope-Hauled Railway

When the Whitby to Pickering railway was built in the 1830s, the engineers had a problem — how to get the railway line from Beck Hole to Goathland. There was a difference in height of some 300 feet (90m) in about one mile (1.5km). It was decided to build a steep incline and haul the carriages to the summit by a rope. Water ballast in tanks would act as the power to raise the carriages. It was a time-consuming job, but speed wasn't essential, otherwise the promoters would not have chosen a horse-powered tramway.

In 1861 the rope broke and wagons ran back down the incline into a goods train. In 1864 the rope broke again and two passengers were killed and thirteen injured. The next year a deviation line was opened around the incline. Seven years later a Leeds-built engine climbed the incline under its own power, but it was later exported to Brazil. The incline now forms part of the Historic Rail Trail between Grosmont and Goathland, a picturesque four mile (6.5km) walk.

Site: follow the Grosmont Rail Trail sign from a gate near Goathland's car park.

Grid Ref: NZ 833014 (North York Moors Touring map)

Volcanic Rock

Volcanoes and the North York Moors may appear at first glance to have little in common. Standing at Sil Howe, north-east of Goathland, you can look along the line of a trench cut into the moors for about a mile (1.5km). This was dug to extract

whinstone. The stones, when broken up into small chippings, are placed on roads to give a hardwearing surface. The stone was formed by volcanic action millions of years ago and lies in a narrow band that stretches across the country.

Eventually, when as much as possible of the stone had been extracted from the surface, a mine adit was driven into the hillside and the mining continued underground. When the stone was brought to the surface, it was placed in railway carriages and pushed downhill to a site above Goathland Station, where the stone was crushed. The wagons were then hauled back up the track by an old car which straddled the railway line. The operation ceased in the 1950s.

Site: to the north of the Sil Howe–Beck Hole road 1¼ miles (2km) north-east of Goathland.

Grid Ref: Sil Howe NZ 851028 (North York Moors Touring map)

No Road to the Village

The valley of the River Esk stretches westwards from Whitby for some twenty miles (32km). Less well known is the hamlet of Esk Valley about half a mile (1km) south of Grosmont. The terraces of houses were built close to the Whitby to Pickering railway, and served the men working at the nearby whinstone mines and the iron mine. Every two weeks a special train was run down the cul-de-sac line from Grosmont to the former Beck Hole Station, delivering groceries, provisions and coal.

In the late 1940s the deteriorating state of the track meant that it would have to close down. But without the railway it was an isolated community, because no road had ever been built into the hamlet. It was not a rich community, but whist drives and cricket matches were organised and supported by the country folk from the surrounding villages. Many enjoyable social occasions finally raised the money for the county council to build a road into the hamlet, which was opened on the 1st October 1951.

Site: signposted off the Goathland—Egton Bridge road, five miles (8km) from Goathland.

Grid Ref: NZ 822043 (North York Moors Touring map)

Father Postgate

The village of Egton Bridge stands beside a picturesque stretch of the River Esk, hemmed in by roads that climb steeply up the valley side. The Postgate Inn at the foot of the steep hill to Egton would appear to be named after some Victorian mail route but it is, in fact, named after Father Postgate, a seventeenth century Roman Catholic priest. Nicholas Postgate was born in the village in 1599 in a cottage near the bridge. In 1621 he went to Douai in France and was ordained a priest in 1629.

On his return to England he served various Yorkshire Catholic families until about 1660, when he returned to the moors serving the area between Whitby and Guisborough. It was a time of religious persecution, and when he was about eighty he was arrested for carrying on the role of a priest. He was taken to York and was convicted. He was hung, drawn and quartered at Tyburn in York in August 1679. His memory is still kept alive today by the Postgate Society.

Site: signposted off the A171 Whitby–Guisborough road, or it can be reached from Goathland.

Grid Ref: NZ 804053 (North York Moors Touring map)

The Road to Nowhere?

Signposts in Goathland offer directions to the Roman Road, which is a walk of about two miles (3km) from the church through fine moorland scenery. For the motorist a much longer, though equally scenic, drive along the Egton Bridge road turning south towards Pickering leads to another section of the Roman Road.

The broad, stoned track strides across the open moorland, clearly displayed for all to see. During 1,900 years of weathering and erosion the top surface has gone, but the road with its stoned foundations can be seen, with side ditches to drain the water. Originally there would have been a top layer of gravel or small stones to give a level surface.

The road came north from the Roman settlement and fort at Malton. It passed Cawthorne Camps (see page 93) and continued over the moors to Lease Rigg above Grosmont. Where it went after that is a mystery. Did it end here? Was there riverborne traffic along the Esk? And if it ended at Lease Rigg, why was it built?

Site: from Goathland, take the unfenced road south past Wheeldale youth hostel and cross the stepping stones, then climb onto the moors.

Grid Ref: Goathland approach SE 807980; Egton Bridge–Pickering road SE 803972 (North York Moors Touring map)

A Roman Service Station?

The hamlet of Stape lies on the edge of the moors and used to supplement its hardy existence by making besoms — the brooms made with dry heather. The last house in the hamlet heading north was the former Hare and Hounds public house. Many years before the Hare and Hounds served ale to locals and passing travellers, the Roman army marched along the road which lies in front. Four hundred yards (360m) northwards along the road is the Old Wives' Well, reached along a signposted forest track.

A square stone trough holds the water, and the well is covered with turf and surrounded by a wooden fence. It lies close to the old Roman road. Did Roman soldiers and other travellers 1,900 years ago pause here for a drink? It was certainly the water supply for Stape for many years.

Site: just off the Newton on Rawcliffe to Egton Bridge road 6½ miles (10km) north of Pickering.

Grid Ref: SE 795940 (North York Moors Touring map)

Further Reading

Rev J C Atkinson, *Forty Years in a Moorland Parish*. Macmillan, 1891.

J B Baker, *The History of Scarborough*. Longmans Green & Co, 1882.

M Boyes, *Exploring The North York Moors*. Dalesman Publishing Co, 1989.

M Boyes & H Chester, *Great Walks North York Moors*. Ward Lock, 1988.

M Boyes & H Chester, *Pickering & Thornton le Dale*. Dalesman Publishing Co, 1991.

M Boyes, *The Crosses Walk*. Dalesman Publishing Co, 1979,

M Boyes, *Walking the Cleveland Way and The Missing Link*. Cicerone Press, 1988.

J Brown & I Croden, *Staithes*. A A Sotheran, 1977.

S K Chapman, *Cleveland Ironstone*. Dalesman Publishing Co, 1973.

A N Cooper, *The Curiosities of East Yorkshire*. A Brown, nd.

J Ford, *Some Reminiscences and Folk Lore of Danby Parish and District*. Horne, 1953.

A Godfrey & P J Lassey, *Shipwrecks of the Yorkshire Coast*. Dalesman Publishing Co, 1974.

F Graham, *Old Inns & Taverns of Yorkshire (North Riding)*. 1965.

G Home, *The Evolution of an English Town*. Dent, 1905.

M Hartley & J Ingilby, *Life and Tradition in the Moorlands of North-East Yorkshire*. Dent, 1972; reprinted Smith Settle, 1990.

R H Hayes, *Old Roads & Pannierways in North East Yorkshire*. North York Moors National Park, 1988.

R H Hayes & J G Rutter, *Rosedale Mines and Railway*. Scarborough & District Archaeological Society, 1974.

R H Hayes & J G Rutter, *Wade's Causeway*. Scarborough & District Archaeological Society, 1964.

A F Humble, *The Rowing Lifeboats of Whitby*. Horne, 1974.

P S Jeffrey, *Whitby Lore and Legend*. Horne, 1952.

D Joy, *Whitby and Pickering Railway*. Dalesman Publishing Co, 1971.

J McDonnell (editor), *A History of Helmsley, Rievaulx and District* Stonegate Press, 1963.

H Mead, *Inside the North York Moors*. Smith Settle, 1994.

Father J Mulholland, *In the Footsteps of Father Postgate*. Postgate Society, 1975.

H Peach, *Discovering East Yorkshire & Humberside*. Smith Settle, 1995.

C Platt, *Abbeys of Yorkshire*. English Heritage, 1988.

J Rushton, *The Ryedale Story*. Ryedale District Council, 1976.

J G Rutter, *Industrial Archaeology in North-East Yorkshire*, vols 1 to 3. Scarborough & District Archaeological Society, 1969.

J Thompson, *The Mouseman of Kilburn*. Dalesman Publishing Co, 1979.

B Wilks, *The Brontës*. Hamlyn, 1975.

Rev G Young, *A History of Whitby and Streoneshalh Abbey*. Caedmon, 1976.

Index